The Gospels Revisited

An Anthology

John Sager

Copyright © 2023 by John Sager

All rights reserved. No part of this book may be reproduced or transmitted in any form or by any means, electronic or mechanical, including photocopying, recording, or any information storage and retrieval system, without permission in writing from the author.

Scripture quotations may be attributed to the
online program Word Search.
The author's comments are in italics.

Library of Congress Control Number: 2023916421

ISBN: 978-1-952483-74-5 (Paperback)
ISBN: 978-1-952483-75-2 (eBook)

Printed in the USA by Book House Publishing
Bellingham, WA

— Also by John Sager —

A Tiffany Monday—an Unusual Love Story, West Bow Press, 2012

Joan's Gallery, 50 Years of Artistry by Joan Johnson Sager, Blurb, Inc. 2013

Uncovered—My Half-Century with the CIA, West Bow Press, 2013

Night Flight, A Novel, CreateSpace, 2013

Operation Night Hawk, A Novel, CreateSpace, 2014

Moscow at Midnight, A Novel, CreateSpace, 2014

The Jihadists' Revenge, A Novel, CreateSpace, 2014

Mole, A Novel, CreateSpace, 2015

Capital Crises, A Novel, CreateSpace, 2015

God's Listeners, An Anthology, CreateSpace, 2015

Crescent Blood, A Novel, CreateSpace, 2016

Sasha—From Stalin to Obama, a Biography, CreateSpace 2016

Shahnoza—Super Spy, A Novel, CreateSpace, 2016

Target Oahu, A Novel, CreateSpace, 2017

Aerosol, A Novel, CreateSpace, 2017

The Health Center, A Novel, CreateSpace, 2017

The Conservator, A Biography, CreateSpace, 2017

The Evil Alliance, A Novel, CreateSpace, 2018

Tehran Revisited, A Novel, Archway Publishers, 2019

St. Barnabas, A Novel, Inspiring Voices, 2019

The Caravan, A Novel, Outskirts Press, 2019

Senator McPherson, A Novel, Inspiring Voices, 2019

Meetings in Moscow, A Novel, Outskirts Press, 2019

Madam President, A Novel, Outskirts Press, 2019

Kiwi Country, A Novel, Outskirts Press, 2020

Inside Iran, A Novel, Outskirts Press, 2020

Introduction

*Most of those of you who will read this story know that for many years I was an employee of the Central Intelligence Agency. As I think back on those years it occurs to me that within the headquarters building's cafeteria there was virtually no chatter about **faith**. I was left to believe that the Bible most likely was written by a group of tired old men, wearing black robes, squatting on their haunches, with nothing else to do but argue with each other, all this in the fifth century, or thereabouts.*

But then something happened. The woman I wanted to marry said she was okay with the marriage idea but for that to happen she told me I should learn something about Jesus Christ and then DO something about it. The woman, about my age and a devout Lutheran believer, introduced me to a few of her male church-goers and I began reading several books, each with a strong apologetics content. After doing all this reading and talking to several men in her congregation, I decided that Christianity is for real. And I was baptized in her church, at age 42.

I was so taken by my new-found faith that I developed a series of PowerPoint presentations, easily projected on a screen with the help of my laptop computer. It is those projections that make up the story you are about to read. And we'll begin at the beginning with Matthew's gospel, the first of the four.

Incidentally, the first three gospels as commonly referred to as the synoptic gospels, because they include the same stories with similar wording, in contrast to the gospel of John, which is relatively unique. Synoptic comes from the Greek words, "syn."

So, what do we know about *this man, Matthew? Here is what my Ryrie Study Bible has to say: Matthew, who was surnamed Levi, was a Jewish tax gatherer for the Roman government. Because he collaborated with the Romans, who were hated by the Jews as overlords of their country, he was despised by fellow Jews. Nevertheless, he responded to Christ's simple call to follow Him. After the account of the banquet he gave for his colleagues so they could meet Jesus, he is not mentioned again except in the list of the twelve.*

Matthew was written to Jews to answer their questions about Jesus of Nazareth who claimed to be their Messiah. Was he in fact the Messiah predicted in the Old Testament? If he was why did he fail to establish the promised kingdom? Will it ever be established? In the meantime, what is God's purpose? As we'll soon see, Matthew begins his gospel with a genealogy, the names of everyone associated with Jesus' birth. And he does this for a reason: he knows that his readers, at that time all of them Jewish, will recognize these names, historical figures of great importance and these names will provide the authenticity for his writing. But we should add that there is another gospel writer, the Apostle John, who was the closest of Jesus of the four, and we can begin with his Gospel.

ONE

Before anything else existed, there was Christ, with God. He has always been alive and is himself God. He created everything there is—nothing exists that he didn't make. Eternal life is in him, and this life gives light to all mankind. His life is the light that shines through the darkness—and the darkness can never extinguish it. God sent John the Baptist as a witness to the fact that Jesus Christ is the true Light.

John himself was not the Light; he was only a witness to identify it. Later on, the one who is the true Light arrived to shine on everyone coming into the world. But although he made the world, the world didn't recognize him when he came. Even in his own land and among his own people, the Jews, he was not accepted. Only a few would welcome and receive him. But to all who received him, he gave the right to become children of God. All they needed to do was to trust him to save them. All those who believe this are reborn!—not a physical rebirth resulting from human passion or plan—but from the will of God. And Christ became a human being and lived here on earth among us and was full of loving forgiveness and truth. And some of us have seen his glory—the glory of the only Son of the heavenly Father! John pointed him out to the people, telling the crowds, "This is the one I was talking about when I said, 'Someone is coming who is greater by far than I am—for he existed long before I did!'" We have all benefited from the rich blessings he brought to us—blessing upon blessing heaped upon us! For Moses gave us only the Law with its rigid demands and merciless justice, while Jesus Christ brought us loving forgiveness as well. No one has ever actually seen God, but, of course, his only Son has, for he is the companion of the Father and has told us all about him.

The Jewish leaders sent priests and assistant priests from Jerusalem to ask John whether he claimed to be the Messiah. He denied it flatly. "I am not the Christ," he said. "Well then, who are you?" they asked. "Are you Elijah?" "No," he replied. "Are you the Prophet?" "No." "Then who are you? Tell us, so we can give an answer to those who sent us. What do you have to say for yourself?" He replied, "I am a voice from the barren wilderness, shouting as Isaiah prophesied, 'Get ready for the coming of the Lord!'" Then those who were sent by the Pharisees asked him, "If you aren't the Messiah or Elijah or the Prophet, what right do you have to baptize?" John told them, "I merely baptize with water, but right here in the crowd is someone you have never met, who will soon begin his ministry among you, and I am not even fit to be his slave." This incident took place at Bethany, a village on the other side of the Jordan River where John was baptizing. The next day John saw Jesus coming toward him and said, "Look! There is the Lamb of God who takes away the world's sin! He is the one I was talking about when I said, 'Soon a man far greater than I am is coming, who existed long before me!' I didn't know he was the one, but I am here baptizing with water in order to point him out to the nation of Israel." Then John told about seeing the Holy Spirit in the form of a dove descending from heaven and resting upon Jesus. "I didn't know he was the one," John said again, "but at the time God sent me to baptize he told me, 'When you see the Holy Spirit descending and resting upon someone—he is the one you are looking for. He is the one who baptizes with the Holy Spirit.' I saw it happen to this man, and I therefore testify that he is the Son of God." The following day as John was standing with two of his disciples, Jesus walked by. John looked at him intently and then declared, "See! There is the Lamb of God!" Then John's two disciples turned and followed Jesus. Jesus looked around and saw them following. "What do you want?" he asked them. "Sir," they replied, "where do you live?" "Come and see," he said. So they went with him to the place where he was staying and were with him from about four o'clock that afternoon until the evening. (One of these men was Andrew, Simon Peter's brother.) Andrew then went to find his brother Peter and told him, "We have found the Messiah!" And he brought Peter to meet Jesus. Jesus looked intently at Peter for a moment and then said, "You are Simon, John's son—but you shall be called Peter, the rock!"

The next day Jesus decided to go to Galilee. He found Philip and told him, "Come with me." (Philip was from Bethsaida, Andrew and Peter's hometown.) Philip now went off to look for Nathanael and told him, "We have found the Messiah!—the very person Moses and the prophets told about! His name is Jesus, the son of Joseph from Nazareth!" "Nazareth!" exclaimed Nathanael. "Can anything good come from there?" "Just come and see for yourself," Philip declared. As they approached, Jesus said, "Here comes an honest man—a true son of Israel." "How do you know what I am like?," Nathanael demanded. And Jesus replied, "I could see you under the fig tree before Philip found you." Nathanael replied, "Sir, you are the Son of God—the King of Israel!" Jesus asked him, "Do you believe all this just because I told you I had seen you under the fig tree? You will see greater proofs than this. You will even see heaven open and the angels of God coming back and forth to me, the Messiah."

Two

These are the ancestors of Jesus Christ, a descendant of King David and of Abraham: Abraham was the father of Isaac; Isaac was the father of Jacob; Jacob was the father of Judah and his brothers. Judah was the father of Perez and Zerah (Tamar was their mother); Perez was the father of Hezron; Hezron was the father of Aram; Aram was the father of Amminadab; Amminadab was the father of Nahshon; Nahshon was the father of Salmon; Salmon was the father of Boaz (Rahab was his mother); Boaz was the father of Obed (Ruth was his mother); Obed was the father of Jesse; Jesse was the father of King David. David was the father of Solomon (his mother was the widow of Uriah); Solomon was the father of Rehoboam; Rehoboam was the father of Abijah; Abijah was the father of Asa; Asa was the father of Jehoshaphat; Jehoshaphat was the father of Joram; Joram was the father of Uzziah; Uzziah was the father of Jotham; Jotham was the father of Ahaz; Ahaz was the father of Hezekiah; Hezekiah was the father of Manasseh; Manasseh was the father of Amos; Amos was the father of Josiah; Josiah was the father of Jechoniah and his brothers (born at the time of the exile to Babylon).

After the exile: Jechoniah was the father of Shealtiel; Shealtiel was the father of Zerubbabel; Zerubbabel was the father of Abiud; Abiud was the father of Eliakim; Eliakim was the father of Azor; Azor was the father of Zadok; Zadok was the father of Achim; Achim was the father of Eliud; Eliud was the father of Eleazar; Eleazar was the father of Matthan; Matthan was the father of Jacob; Jacob was the father of Joseph (who was the husband of Mary, the mother of Jesus Christ the Messiah). These are fourteen of the generations from Abraham to King David; and fourteen from King David's time to the exile; and fourteen from the exile to Christ.

THESE ARE THE FACTS CONCERNING THE birth of Jesus Christ: His mother, Mary, was engaged to be married to Joseph. But while she was still a virgin she became pregnant by the Holy Spirit. Then Joseph, her fiancé, being a man of stern principle, decided to break the engagement but to do it quietly, as he didn't want to publicly disgrace her. As he lay awake considering this, he fell into a dream, and saw an angel standing beside him. "Joseph, son of David," the angel said, "don't hesitate to take Mary as your wife! For the child within her has been conceived by the Holy Spirit. And she will have a Son, and you shall name him Jesus (meaning 'Savior'), for he will save his people from their sins. This will fulfill God's message through his prophets—*'Listen! The virgin shall conceive a child!* She shall give birth to a Son, and he shall be called 'Emmanuel' (meaning 'God is with us')."" When Joseph awoke, he did as the angel commanded and brought Mary home to be his wife, but she remained a virgin until her Son was born; and Joseph named him "Jesus."

NOW THE BIRTH OF JESUS CHRIST was as follows: when His mother Mary had been betrothed to Joseph, before they came together she was found to be with child by the Holy Spirit. And

Joseph her husband, being a righteous man and not wanting to disgrace her, planned to send her away secretly. But when he had considered this, behold, an angel of the Lord appeared to him in a dream, saying, "Joseph, son of David, do not be afraid to take Mary as your wife; for the Child who has been conceived in her is of the Holy Spirit. She will bear a Son; and you shall call His name Jesus, for He will save His people from their sins."

Now all this took place to fulfill what was spoken by the Lord through the prophet: "BEHOLD, THE VIRGIN SHALL BE WITH CHILD AND SHALL BEAR A SON, AND THEY SHALL CALL HIS NAME IMMANUEL," which translated means, "GOD WITH US." And Joseph awoke from his sleep and did as the angel of the Lord commanded him, and took *Mary* as his wife, but kept her a virgin until she gave birth to a Son; and he called His name Jesus.

THAT'S AS FAR AS WE'LL GO with this introduction to Matthew's gospel. It will appear at the end of this story as perhaps the most important words ever spoken by Jesus. But for now, let's peruse the second of the four gospels, the one written by Mark.

Here begins the wonderful story of Jesus the Messiah, the Son of God. In the book written by the prophet Isaiah, God announced that he would send his Son to earth, and that a special messenger would arrive first to prepare the world for his coming. "This messenger will live out in the barren wilderness," Isaiah said, "and will proclaim that everyone must straighten out his life to be ready for the Lord's arrival." This messenger was John the Baptist. He lived in the wilderness and taught that all should be baptized as a public announcement of their decision to turn their backs on sin, so that God could forgive them. People from Jerusalem and from all over Judea traveled out into the Judean wastelands to see and hear John, and when they confessed their sins he baptized them in the Jordan River. His clothes were woven from camel's hair and he wore a leather belt; locusts and wild honey were his food. Here is a sample of his preaching: "Someone is coming soon who is far greater than I am, so much greater that I am not even worthy to be his slave. I baptize you with water but he will baptize you with God's Holy Spirit!" Then one day Jesus came from Nazareth in Galilee, and was baptized by John there in the Jordan River. The moment Jesus came up out of the water, he saw the heavens open and the Holy Spirit in the form of a dove descending on him, and a voice from heaven said, "You are my beloved Son; you are my Delight." Immediately the Holy Spirit urged Jesus into the desert. There, for forty days, alone except for desert animals, he was subjected to Satan's temptations to sin. And afterwards the angels came and cared for him. Later on, after John was arrested by King Herod, Jesus went to Galilee to preach God's Good News. "At last the time has come!," he announced. "God's Kingdom is near! Turn from your sins and act on this glorious news!"

One day as Jesus was walking along the shores of the Sea of Galilee, he saw Simon and his brother Andrew fishing with nets, for they were commercial fishermen. Jesus called out to them, "Come, follow me! And I will make you fishermen for the souls of men!" At once they left their nets and went along with him. A little farther up the beach, he saw Zebedee's sons, James and John, in a boat mending their nets. He called them too, and immediately they left their father Zebedee in the boat with the hired men and went with him. Jesus and his companions now arrived at the town of Capernaum and on Saturday morning went into the Jewish place of worship—the synagogue—where he preached. The congregation was surprised at his sermon because he spoke as an authority and didn't try to prove his points by quoting others—quite unlike what they were used to hearing! A man possessed by a demon was present and began shouting, "Why are you bothering us, Jesus of Nazareth—have you come to destroy us demons? I know who you are—the holy Son of God!" Jesus curtly commanded the demon to say no more and to come out of the man. At that the evil spirit screamed and convulsed the man violently and left him. Amazement gripped the audience and they began discussing what had happened. "What sort of new religion is this?," they asked excitedly. "Why, even evil spirits obey his orders!" The news of what he had done spread quickly through that entire area of Galilee. Then, leaving the synagogue, he and his disciples went over to Simon and Andrew's home, where they found Simon's mother-in-law sick in bed with a high fever. They told Jesus about her right away. He went to her bedside, and as he took her by the hand and helped her to sit up, the fever suddenly left, and she got up and prepared dinner for them! By sunset the courtyard was filled with the sick and demon-possessed, brought to him for healing; and a huge crowd of people from all over the city of Capernaum gathered outside the door to watch. So Jesus healed great numbers of sick folk that evening and ordered many demons to come out of their victims. (But he refused to allow the demons to speak, because they knew who he was.) The next morning he was up long before daybreak and went out alone into the wilderness to pray. Later, Simon and the others went out to find him, and told him, "Everyone is asking for you." But he replied, "We must go on to other towns as well, and give my message to them too, for that is why I came." So he traveled throughout the province of Galilee, preaching in the synagogues and releasing many from the power of demons.

Once a leper came and knelt in front of him and begged to be healed. "If you want to, you can make me well again," he pled. And Jesus, moved with pity, touched him and said, "I want to! Be healed!" Immediately the leprosy was gone—the man was healed! Jesus then told him sternly, "Go and be examined immediately by the Jewish priest. Don't stop to speak to anyone along the way.

Take along the offering prescribed by Moses for a leper who is healed, so that everyone will have proof that you are well again." But as the man went on his way he began to shout the good news that he was healed; as a result, such throngs soon surrounded Jesus that he couldn't publicly enter a city anywhere, but had to stay out in the barren wastelands. And people from everywhere came to him there.

Three

Several days later he returned to Capernaum, the news of his arrival spread quickly through the city. Soon the house where he was staying was so packed with visitors that there wasn't room for a single person more, not even outside the door. And he preached the Word to them. Four men arrived carrying a paralyzed man on a stretcher. They couldn't get to Jesus through the crowd, so they dug through the clay roof above his head and lowered the sick man on his stretcher, right down in front of Jesus. When Jesus saw how strongly they believed that he would help, Jesus said to the sick man, "Son, your sins are forgiven!" But some of the Jewish religious leaders said to themselves as they sat there, "What? This is blasphemy! Does he think he is God? For only God can forgive sins." Jesus could read their minds and said to them at once, "Why does this bother you? I, the Messiah, have the authority on earth to forgive sins. But talk is cheap—anybody could say that. So I'll prove it to you by healing this man." Then, turning to the paralyzed man, he commanded, "Pick up your stretcher and go on home, for you are healed!" The man jumped up, took the stretcher, and pushed his way through the stunned onlookers! Then how they praised God. "We've never seen anything like this before!," they all exclaimed.

THEN JESUS WENT OUT TO THE seashore again and preached to the crowds that gathered around him. As he was walking up the beach he saw Levi, the son of Alphaeus, sitting at his tax collection booth. "Come with me," Jesus told him. "Come be my disciple." And Levi jumped to his feet and went along. That night Levi invited his fellow tax collectors and many other notorious sinners to be his dinner guests so that they could meet Jesus and his disciples. (There were many men of this type among the crowds that followed him.) But when some of the Jewish religious leaders saw him eating with these men of ill repute, they said to his disciples, "How can he stand it, to eat with such scum?" When Jesus heard what they were saying, he told them, "Sick people need the doctor, not healthy ones! I haven't come to tell good people to repent, but the bad ones." John's disciples and the Jewish leaders sometimes fasted, that is, went without food as part of their religion. One day some people came to Jesus and asked why his disciples didn't do this too. Jesus replied, "Do friends of the bridegroom refuse to eat at the wedding feast? Should they be sad while he is with them? But some day he will be taken away from them, and then they will mourn. [Besides, going without food is part of the old way of doing things.] It is like patching an old garment with unshrunk cloth! What happens? The patch pulls away and leaves the hole worse than before. You know better than to put new wine into old wineskins. They would burst. The wine would be spilled out and the wineskins ruined. New wine needs fresh wineskins."

Another time, on a Sabbath day as Jesus and his disciples were walking through the fields, the disciples were breaking off heads of wheat and eating the grain. Some of the Jewish religious leaders said to Jesus, "They shouldn't be doing that! It's against our laws to work by harvesting grain on the Sabbath." But Jesus replied, "Didn't you ever hear about the time King David and his companions were hungry, and he went into the house of God—Abiathar was High Priest then—and they ate the special bread only priests were allowed to eat? That was against the law too. But the Sabbath was made to benefit man, and not man to benefit the Sabbath. And I, the Messiah, have authority even to decide what men can do on Sabbath days!"

WHILE IN CAPERNAUM JESUS WENT OVER to the synagogue again, and noticed a man there with a deformed hand. Since it was the Sabbath, Jesus' enemies watched him closely. Would he heal the man's hand? If he did, they planned to arrest him! Jesus asked the man to come and stand in front of the congregation. Then turning to his enemies he asked, "Is it all right to do kind deeds on Sabbath days? Or is this a day for doing harm? Is it a day to save lives or to destroy them?" But they wouldn't answer him. Looking around at them angrily, for he was deeply disturbed by their indifference to human need, he said to the man, "Reach out your hand." He did, and instantly his hand was healed! At once the Pharisees went away and met with the Herodians to discuss plans for killing Jesus. Meanwhile, Jesus and his disciples withdrew to the beach, followed by a huge crowd from all over Galilee, Judea, Jerusalem, Idumea, from beyond the Jordan River, and even from as far away as Tyre and Sidon. For the news about his miracles had spread far and wide and vast numbers came to see him for themselves. He instructed his disciples to bring around a boat and to have it standing ready to rescue him in case he was crowded off the beach. For there had been many healings that day and as a result great numbers of sick people were crowding around him, trying to touch him. And whenever those possessed by demons caught sight of him they would fall down before him shrieking, "You are the Son of God!" But he strictly warned them not to make him known.

Afterwards he went up into the hills and summoned certain ones he chose, inviting them to come and join him there; and they did. Then he selected twelve of them to be his regular companions and to go out to preach and to cast out demons.

These are the names of the twelve he chose: Simon (he renamed him "Peter"), James and John (the sons of Zebedee, but Jesus called them "Sons of Thunder"), Andrew, Philip, Bartholomew, Matthew, Thomas, James (the son of Alphaeus), Thaddaeus, Simon (a member of a political party advocating violent overthrow of the Roman government), Judas Iscariot (who later betrayed him).

When he returned to the house where he was staying, the crowds began to gather again, and soon it was so full of visitors that he couldn't even find time to eat. When his friends heard what was happening they came to try to take him home with them. "He's out of his mind," they said. But the Jewish teachers of religion who had arrived from Jerusalem said, "His trouble is that he's possessed by Satan, king of demons. That's why demons obey him." Jesus summoned these men and asked them (using proverbs they all understood), "How can Satan cast out Satan? A kingdom divided against itself will collapse. A home filled with strife and division destroys itself. And if Satan is fighting against himself, how can he accomplish anything? He would never survive. [Satan must be bound before his demons are cast out], just as a strong man must be tied up before his house can be ransacked and his property robbed. I solemnly declare that any sin of man can be forgiven, even blasphemy against me; but blasphemy against the Holy Spirit can never be forgiven. It is an eternal sin." He told them this because they were saying he did his miracles by Satan's power [instead of acknowledging it was by the Holy Spirit's power]. Now his mother and brothers arrived at the crowded house where he was teaching, and they sent word for him to come out and talk with them. "Your mother and brothers are outside and want to see you," he was told. He replied, "Who is my mother? Who are my brothers?" Looking at those around him he said, "These are my mother and brothers! Anyone who does God's will is my brother, and my sister, and my mother."

WHILE IN CAPERNAUM JESUS WENT OVER to the synagogue again, and noticed a man there with a deformed hand. Since it was the Sabbath, Jesus' enemies watched him closely. Would he heal the man's hand? If he did, they planned to arrest him! Jesus asked the man to come and stand in front of the congregation. Then turning to his enemies he asked, "Is it all right to do kind deeds on Sabbath days? Or is this a day for doing harm? Is it a day to save lives or to destroy them?" But they wouldn't answer him. Looking around at them angrily, for he was deeply disturbed by their indifference to human need, he said to the man, "Reach out your hand." He did, and instantly his hand was healed! At once the Pharisees went away and met with the Herodians to discuss plans for killing Jesus. Meanwhile, Jesus and his disciples withdrew to the beach, followed by a huge crowd from all over Galilee, Judea, Jerusalem, Idumea, from beyond the Jordan River, and even from as far away as Tyre and Sidon. For the news about his miracles had spread far and wide and vast numbers came to see him for themselves. He instructed his disciples to bring around a boat and to have it standing ready to rescue him in case he was crowded off the beach. For there had been many healings that day and as a result great numbers of sick people were crowding around him, trying to touch him. And whenever those possessed by demons caught sight of him they would fall down before him shrieking, "You are the Son of God!" But he strictly warned them not to make him known. Afterwards he went up into the hills and summoned certain ones he chose, inviting them to come and join him there; and they did. Then he selected twelve of them to be his regular companions and to go out to preach and to cast out demons. These are the names of the twelve he chose: Simon (he renamed him "Peter"), James and John (the sons of Zebedee, but Jesus called them "Sons of Thunder"), Andrew, Philip, Bartholomew, Matthew, Thomas, James (the son of Alphaeus), Thaddaeus, Simon (a member of a political party advocating violent overthrow of the Roman government) and Judas Iscariot (who later betrayed him).

When he returned to the house where he was staying, the crowds began to gather again, and soon it was so full of visitors that he couldn't even find time to eat. When his friends heard what was happening they came to try to take him home with them. "He's out of his mind," they said. But the Jewish teachers of religion who had arrived from Jerusalem said, "His trouble is that he's possessed by Satan, king of demons. That's why demons obey him." Jesus summoned these men and asked them (using proverbs they all understood), "How can Satan cast out Satan? A kingdom divided against itself will collapse. A home filled with strife and division destroys itself. And if Satan is fighting against himself, how can he accomplish anything? He would never survive.[Satan must be bound before his demons are cast out, just as a strong man must be tied up before his house can be ransacked and his property robbed. I solemnly declare that any sin of man can be forgiven, even blasphemy against me; but blasphemy against the Holy Spirit can never be forgiven. It is an eternal sin." He told them this because they were saying he did his miracles by Satan's power [instead of acknowledging it was by the Holy Spirit's power]. Now his mother and brothers arrived at the crowded house where he was teaching, and they sent word for him to come out and talk with them. "Your mother and brothers are outside and want to see you," he was told. He replied, "Who is my mother? Who are my brothers?" Looking at those around him he said, "These are my mother and brothers! Anyone who does God's will is my brother, and my sister, and my mother."

Four

Once again an immense crowd gathered around him on the beach as he was teaching, so he got into a boat and sat down and talked from there. His usual method of teaching was to tell the people stories. One of them went like this: "Listen! A farmer decided to sow some grain. As he scattered it across his field, some of it fell on a path, and the birds came and picked it off the hard ground and ate it. Some fell on thin soil with underlying rock. It grew up quickly enough, but soon wilted beneath the hot sun and died because the roots had no nourishment in the shallow soil among thorns that shot up and crowded the young plants so that they produced no grain. But some of the seeds fell into good soil and yielded thirty times as much as he had planted—some of it even sixty or a hundred times as much! If you have ears, listen!"

Afterwards, when he was alone with the twelve and with his other disciples, they asked him, "What does your story mean?" He replied, "You are permitted to know some truths about the Kingdom of God that are hidden to those outside the Kingdom:

Though they see and hear, they will not understand or turn to God, or be forgiven for their sins. But if you can't understand *this* simple illustration, what will you do about all the others I am going to tell? The farmer I talked about is anyone who brings God's message to others, trying to plant good seed within their lives. The hard pathway, where some of the seed fell, represents the hard hearts of some of those who hear God's message; Satan comes at once to try to make them forget it. The rocky soil represents the hearts of those who hear the message with joy, but, like young plants in such soil, their roots don't go very deep, and though at first they get along fine, as soon as persecution begins, they wilt. The thorny ground represents the hearts of people who listen to the Good News and receive it, but all too quickly the attractions of this world and the delights of wealth, and the search for success and lure of nice things come in and crowd out God's message from their hearts, so that no crop is produced. But the good soil represents the hearts of those who truly accept God's message and produce a plentiful harvest for God—thirty, sixty, or even a hundred times as much as was planted in their hearts."

Then he asked them, "When someone lights a lamp, does he put a box over it to shut out the light? Of course not! The light couldn't be seen or used. A lamp is placed on a stand to shine and be useful. All that is now hidden will someday come to light. If you have ears, listen! And be sure to put into practice what you hear. The more you do this, the more you will understand what I tell you. To him who has shall be given; from him who has not shall be taken away even what he has."

Here is another story illustrating what the Kingdom of God is like: "A farmer sowed his field and went away, and as the days went by, the seeds grew and grew without his help. For the soil made the seeds grow. First a leaf-blade pushed through, and later the wheat-heads formed and finally the grain ripened, and then the farmer came at once with his sickle and harvested it." Jesus asked, "How can I describe the Kingdom of God? What story shall I use to illustrate it? It is like a tiny mustard seed! Though this is one of the smallest of seeds, yet it grows to become one of the largest of plants, with long branches where birds can build their nests and be sheltered." He used many such illustrations to teach the people as much as they were ready to understand. In fact, he taught only by illustrations in his public teaching, but afterwards, when he was alone with his disciples, he would explain his meaning to them.

As evening fell, Jesus said to his disciples, "Let's cross to the other side of the lake." So they took him just as he was and started out, leaving the crowds behind (though other boats followed). But soon a terrible storm arose. High waves began to break into the boat until it was nearly full of water and about to sink. Jesus was asleep at the back of the boat with his head on a cushion. Frantically they wakened him, shouting, "Teacher, don't you even care that we are all about to drown?" Then he rebuked the wind and said to the sea, "Quiet down!" And the wind fell, and there was a great calm! And he asked them, "Why were you so fearful? Don't you even yet have confidence in me?" And they were filled with awe and said among themselves, "Who is this man, that even the winds and seas obey him?"

When they arrived at the other side of the lake, a demon-possessed man ran out from a graveyard, just as Jesus was climbing from the boat. This man lived among the gravestones and had such strength that whenever he was put into handcuffs and shackles—as he often was—he snapped the handcuffs from his wrists and smashed the shackles and walked away. No one was strong enough to control him. All day long and through the night he would wander among the tombs and in the wild hills, screaming and cutting himself with sharp pieces of stone. When Jesus was still far out on the water, the man had seen him and had run to meet him, and fell down before him. Then Jesus spoke to the demon within the man and said, "Come out, you evil spirit." It gave a terrible scream, shrieking, "What are you going to do to me, Jesus, Son of the Most High God? For God's sake, don't torture me!" "What is your name?," Jesus asked, and the demon replied, "Legion, for there are many of us here within this man." Then the demons begged him again and again not to send them to some distant land.

Now as it happened there was a huge herd of hogs rooting around on the hill above the lake. "Send us into those hogs," the demons begged. And Jesus gave them permission. Then the evil spirits came out of the man and entered the hogs, and the entire herd plunged down the steep hillside into the lake and drowned. The herdsmen fled to the nearby towns and countryside, spreading the news as they ran. Everyone rushed out to see for themselves. And a large crowd soon gathered where Jesus was; but as they saw the man sitting there, fully clothed and perfectly sane, they were frightened. Those who saw what happened were telling everyone about it, and the crowd began pleading with Jesus to go away and leave them alone! So he got back into the boat. The man who had been possessed by the demons begged Jesus to let him go along. But Jesus said no. "Go home to your friends," he told him, "and tell them what wonderful things God has done for you; and how merciful he has been." So the man started off to visit the Ten Towns of that region and began to tell everyone about the great things Jesus had done for him; and they were awestruck by his story.

When Jesus had gone across by boat to the other side of the lake, a vast crowd gathered around him on the shore. The leader of the local synagogue, whose name was Jairus, came and fell down before him, pleading with him to heal his little daughter. "She is at the point of death," he said in desperation. "Please come and place your hands on her and make her live." Jesus went with him, and the crowd thronged behind. In the crowd was a woman who had been sick for twelve years with a hemorrhage. She had suffered much from many doctors through the years and had become poor from paying them, and was no better but, in fact, was worse.

She had heard all about the wonderful miracles Jesus did, and that is why she came up behind him through the crowd and touched his clothes. For she thought to herself, "If I can just touch his clothing, I will be healed." And sure enough, as soon as she had touched him, the bleeding stopped and she knew she was well! Jesus realized at once that healing power had gone out from him, so he turned around in the crowd and asked, "Who touched my clothes?" His disciples said to him, "All this crowd pressing around you, and you ask who touched you?" But he kept on looking around to see who it was who had done it. Then the frightened woman, trembling at the realization of what had happened to her, came and fell at his feet and told him what she had done. And he said to her, "Daughter, your faith has made you well; go in peace, healed of your disease."

While he was still talking to her, messengers arrived from Jairus' home with the news that it was too late—his daughter was dead and there was no point in Jesus' coming now. But Jesus ignored their comments and said to Jairus, "Don't be afraid. Just trust me." Then Jesus halted the crowd and wouldn't let anyone go on with him to Jairus' home except Peter and James and John.

When they arrived, Jesus saw that all was in great confusion, with unrestrained weeping and wailing. He went inside and spoke to the people. "Why all this weeping and commotion?," he asked. "The child isn't dead; she is only asleep!" They laughed at him in bitter derision, but he told them all to leave, and taking the little girl's father and mother and his three disciples, he went into the room where she was lying. Taking her by the hand he said to her, "Get up, little girl!" (She was twelve years old.) And she jumped up and walked around! Her parents just couldn't get over it. Jesus instructed them very earnestly not to tell what had happened and told them to give her something to eat.

Soon afterwards he left that section of the country and returned with his disciples to Nazareth, his hometown. The next Sabbath he went to the synagogue to teach, and the people were astonished at his wisdom and his miracles because he was just a local man like themselves. "He's no better than we are," they said. "He's just a carpenter, Mary's boy, and a brother of James and Joseph, Judas and Simon. And his sisters live right here among us." And they were offended! Then Jesus told them, "A prophet is honored everywhere except in his hometown and among his relatives and by his own family." And because of their unbelief he couldn't do any mighty miracles among them except to place his hands on a few sick people and heal them. And he could hardly accept the fact that they wouldn't believe in him. Then he went out among the villages, teaching. And he called his twelve disciples together and sent them out two by two, with power to cast out demons. He told them to take nothing with them except their walking sticks—no food, no knapsack, no money, not even an extra pair of shoes or a change of clothes. "Stay at one home in each village—don't shift around from house to house while you are there," he said. "And whenever a village won't accept you or listen to you, shake off the dust from your feet as you leave; it is a sign that you have abandoned it to its fate." So the disciples went out, telling everyone they met to turn from sin. And they cast out many demons and healed many sick people, anointing them with olive oil.

King Herod soon heard about Jesus, for his miracles were talked about everywhere. The king thought Jesus was John the Baptist come back to life again. So the people were saying, "No wonder he can do such miracles."

Others thought Jesus was Elijah the ancient prophet, now returned to life again; still others claimed he was a new prophet like the great ones of the past. "No," Herod said, "it is John, the man I beheaded. He has come back from the dead." For Herod had sent soldiers to arrest and imprison John because he kept saying it was wrong for the king to marry Herodias, his brother Philip's wife. Herodias wanted John killed in revenge, but without Herod's approval she was powerless. And Herod respected John, knowing that he was a good and holy man, and so he kept him under his protection. Herod was disturbed whenever he talked with John, but even so he liked to listen to him. Herodias' chance finally came. It was Herod's birthday and he gave a stag party for his palace aides, army officers, and the leading citizens of Galilee. Then Herodias' daughter came in and danced before them and greatly pleased them all. "Ask me for anything you like," the king vowed, "even half of my kingdom, and I will give it to you!" She went out and consulted her mother, who told her, "Ask for John the Baptist's head!" So she hurried back to the king and told him, "I want the head of John the Baptist—right now—on a tray!" Then the king was sorry, but he was embarrassed to break his oath in front of his guests. So he sent one of his bodyguards to the prison to cut off John's head and bring it to him. The soldier killed John in the prison, and brought back his head on a tray, and gave it to the girl and she took it to her mother.

When John's disciples heard what had happened, they came for his body and buried it in a tomb.

THE APOSTLES NOW RETURNED TO JESUS from their tour and told him all they had done and what they had said to the people they visited. Then Jesus suggested, "Let's get away from the crowds for a while and rest." For so many people were coming and going that they scarcely had time to eat.

So they left by boat for a quieter spot. But many people saw them leaving and ran on ahead along the shore and met them as they landed. So the usual vast crowd was there as he stepped from the boat; and he had pity on them because they were like sheep without a shepherd, and he taught them many things they needed to know. Late in the afternoon his disciples came to him and said, "Tell the people to go away to the nearby villages and farms and buy themselves some food, for there is nothing to eat here in this desolate spot, and it is getting late."

But Jesus said, *"You* feed them." "With what?" they asked. "It would take a fortune to buy food for all this crowd!" "How much food do we have?" he asked. "Go and find out." They came back to report that there were five loaves of bread and two fish. Then Jesus told the crowd to sit down, and soon colorful groups of fifty or a hundred each were sitting on the green grass. He took the five loaves and two fish and looking up to heaven, gave thanks for the food. Breaking the loaves into pieces, he gave some of the bread and fish to each disciple to place before the people. And the crowd ate until they could hold no more! There were about 5,000 men there for that meal, and afterwards twelve basketfuls of scraps were picked up off the grass!

Immediately after this Jesus instructed his disciples to get back into the boat and strike out across the lake to Bethsaida, where he would join them later. He himself would stay and tell the crowds good-bye and get them started home.

Afterwards he went up into the hills to pray. During the night, as the disciples in their boat were out in the middle of the lake, and he was alone on land, he saw that they were in serious trouble, rowing hard and struggling against the wind and waves. About three o'clock in the morning he walked out to them on the water. He started past them, but when they saw something walking along beside them they screamed in terror, thinking it was a ghost, for they all saw him. But he spoke to them at once. "It's all right," he said. "It is I! Don't be afraid." Then he climbed into the boat and the wind stopped! They just sat there, unable to take it in! For they still didn't realize who he was, even after the miracle the evening before! For they didn't want to believe! When they arrived at Gennesaret on the other side of the lake, they moored the boat and climbed out. The people standing around there recognized him at once, and ran throughout the whole area to spread the news of his arrival, and began carrying sick folks to him on mats and stretchers. Wherever he went—in villages and cities, and out on the farms—they laid the sick in the market plazas and streets, and begged him to let them at least touch the fringes of his clothes; and as many as touched him were healed.

One day some Jewish religious leaders arrived from Jerusalem to investigate him, and noticed that some of his disciples failed to follow the usual Jewish rituals before eating. (For the Jews, especially the Pharisees, will never eat until they have sprinkled their arms to the elbows, as required by their ancient traditions. So when they come home from the market they must always sprinkle themselves in this way before touching any food. This is but one of many examples of laws and regulations they have clung to for centuries, and still follow, such as their ceremony of cleansing for pots, pans and dishes.) So the religious leaders asked him, "Why don't your disciples follow our age-old customs? For they eat without first performing the washing ceremony." Jesus replied, "You bunch of hypocrites! Isaiah the prophet described you very well when he said, 'These people speak very prettily about the Lord but they have no love for him at all. Their worship is a farce, for they claim that God commands the people to obey their petty rules.' How right Isaiah was! For you ignore God's specific orders and substitute your own traditions. You are simply rejecting God's laws and trampling them under your feet for the sake of tradition. For instance, Moses gave you this law from God: 'Honor your father and mother.' And he said that anyone who speaks against his father or mother must die. But you say it is perfectly all right for a man to disregard his needy parents, telling them, 'Sorry, I can't help you! For I have given to God what I could have given to you.' And so you break the law of God in order to protect your man-made tradition. And this is only one example. There are many, many others." Then Jesus called to the crowd to come and hear. "All of you listen," he said, "and try to understand. Your souls aren't harmed by what you eat, but by what you think and say!" Then he went into a house to get away from the crowds, and his disciples asked him what he meant by the statement he had just made. "Don't you understand either?," he asked. "Can't you see that what you eat won't harm your soul? For food doesn't come in contact with your heart, but only passes through the digestive system." (By saying this he showed that every kind of food is kosher.) And then he added, "It is the thought-life that pollutes. For from within, out of men's hearts, come evil thoughts of lust, theft, murder, adultery, wanting what belongs to others, wickedness, deceit, lewdness, envy, slander, pride, and all other folly. All these vile things come from within; they are what pollute you and make you unfit for God."

Then he left Galilee and went to the region of Tyre and Sidon, and tried to keep it a secret that he was there, but couldn't. For as usual the news of his arrival spread fast. Right away a woman came to him whose little girl was possessed by a demon. She had heard about Jesus and now she came and fell at his feet, and pled with him to release her child from the demon's control. Jesus told her, "First I should help my own family—the Jews. It isn't right to take the children's food and throw it to the dogs." She replied, "That's true, sir, but even the puppies under the table are given some scraps from the children's plates." "Good!," he said. "You have answered well—so well that I have healed your little girl. Go on home, for the demon has left her!" And when she arrived home, her little girl was lying quietly in bed, and the demon was gone. From Tyre he went to Sidon, then back to the Sea of Galilee by way of the Ten Towns. A deaf man with a speech impediment was brought to him, and everyone begged Jesus to lay his hands on the man and heal him. Jesus led him away from the crowd and put his fingers into the man's ears, then spat and touched the man's tongue with the spittle. Then, looking up to heaven, he sighed and commanded, "Open!" Instantly the man could hear perfectly and speak plainly! Jesus told the crowd not to spread the news, but the more he forbade them, the more they made it known, for they were overcome with utter amazement. Again and again they said, "Everything he does is wonderful; he even corrects deafness and stammering!"

ONE DAY ABOUT THIS TIME as another great crowd gathered, the people ran out of food again. Jesus called his disciples to discuss the situation. "I pity these people," he said, "for they have been here three days and have nothing left to eat. And if I send them home without feeding them, they will faint along the road! For some of them have come a long distance." "Are we supposed to find food for them here in the desert?," his disciples scoffed. "How many loaves of bread do you have?," he asked. "Seven," they replied. So he told the crowd to sit down on the ground. Then he took the seven loaves, thanked God for them, broke them into pieces and passed them to his disciples; and the disciples placed them before the people. A few small fish were found, too, so Jesus also blessed these and told the disciples to serve them. And the whole crowd ate until they were full, and afterwards he sent them home. There were about 4,000 people in the crowd that day and when the scraps were picked up after the meal, there were seven very large basketfuls left over! Immediately after this he got into a boat with his disciples and came to the region of Dalmanutha. When the local Jewish leaders learned of his arrival, they came to argue with him. "Do a miracle for us," they said. "Make something happen in the sky. Then we will believe in you." He sighed deeply when he heard this and he said, "Certainly not. How many more miracles do you people need?" So he got back into the boat and left them, and crossed to the other side of the lake. But the disciples had forgotten to stock up on food before they left and had only one loaf of bread in the boat.

As they were crossing, Jesus said to them very solemnly, "Beware of the yeast of King Herod and of the Pharisees." "What does he mean?," the disciples asked each other. They finally decided that he must be talking about their forgetting to bring bread. Jesus realized what they were discussing and said, "No, that isn't it at all! Can't you understand? Are your hearts too hard to take it in? Your eyes are to see with—why don't you look? Why don't you open your ears and listen? Don't you remember anything at all? What about the 5,000 men I fed with five loaves of bread? How many basketfuls of scraps did you pick up afterwards?" "Twelve," they said. "And when I fed the 4,000 with seven loaves, how much was left?" "Seven basketfuls," they said. "And yet you think I'm worried that we have no bread?"

When they arrived at Bethsaida, some people brought a blind man to him and begged him to touch and heal him. Jesus took the blind man by the hand and led him out of the village, and spat upon his eyes, and laid his hands over them. "Can you see anything now?," Jesus asked him. The man looked around. "Yes!," he said, "I see men! But I can't see them very clearly; they look like tree trunks walking around!" Then Jesus placed his hands over the man's eyes again and as the man stared intently, his sight was completely restored, and he saw everything clearly, drinking in the sights around him. Jesus sent him home to his family. "Don't even go back to the village first," he said.

Jesus and his disciples now left Galilee and went out to the villages of Caesarea Philippi. As they were walking along he asked them, "Who do the people think I am? What are they saying about me?" "Some of them think you are John the Baptist," the disciples replied, "and others say you are Elijah or some other ancient prophet come back to life again." Then he asked, "Who do you think I am?" Peter replied, "You are the Messiah." But Jesus warned them not to tell anyone! Then he began to tell them about the terrible things he would suffer, and that he would be rejected by the elders and the Chief Priests and the other Jewish leaders—and be killed, and that he would rise again three days afterwards. He talked about it quite frankly with them, so Peter took him aside and chided him. "You shouldn't say things like that," he told Jesus. Jesus turned and looked at his disciples and then said to Peter very sternly, "Satan, get behind me! You are looking at this only from a human point of view and not from God's." Then he called his disciples and the crowds to come over and listen. "If any of you wants to be my follower," he told them, "you must put aside your own pleasures and shoulder your cross, and follow me closely. If you insist on saving your life, you will lose it. Only those who throw away their lives for my sake and for the sake of the Good News will ever know what it means to really live. And how does a man benefit if he gains the whole world and loses his soul in the process? For is anything worth more than his soul? And anyone who is ashamed of me and my message in these days of unbelief and sin, I, the Messiah, will be ashamed of him when I return in the glory of my Father, with the holy angels."

Jesus went on to say to his disciples, "Some of you who are standing here right now will live to see the Kingdom of God arrive in great power!" Six days later Jesus took Peter, James and John to the top of a mountain. No one else was there. Suddenly his face began to shine with glory, and his clothing became dazzling white, far more glorious than any earthly process could ever make it! Then Elijah and Moses appeared and began talking with Jesus! "Teacher, this is wonderful!," Peter exclaimed. "We will make three shelters here, one for each of you . . ." He said this just to be talking, for he didn't know what else to say and they were all terribly frightened. But while he was still speaking these words, a cloud covered them, blotting out the sun, and a voice from the cloud said, "This is my beloved Son. Listen to him." Then suddenly they looked around and Moses and Elijah were gone, and only Jesus was with them. As they descended the mountainside he told them never to mention what they had seen until after he had risen from the dead. So they kept it to themselves, but often talked about it, and wondered what he meant by "rising from the dead." Now they began asking him about something the Jewish religious leaders often spoke of, that Elijah must return before the Messiah could come. Jesus agreed that Elijah must come first and prepare the way—and that he had, in fact, already come! And that he had been terribly mistreated, just as the prophets had predicted. Then Jesus asked them what the prophets could have been talking about when they predicted that the Messiah would suffer and be treated with utter contempt. At the bottom of the mountain they found a great crowd surrounding the other nine disciples, as some Jewish leaders argued with them. The crowd watched Jesus in awe as he came toward them, and then ran to greet him. "What's all the argument about?," he asked. One of the men in the crowd spoke up and said, "Teacher, I brought my son for you to heal—he can't talk because he is possessed by a demon. And whenever the demon is in control of him it dashes him to the ground and makes him foam at the mouth and grind his teeth and become rigid. So I begged your disciples to cast out the demon, but they couldn't do it." Jesus said [to his disciples], "Oh, what tiny faith you have; how much longer must I be with you until you believe? How much longer must I be patient with you? Bring the boy to me." So they brought the boy, but when he saw Jesus the demon convulsed the child horribly, and he fell to the ground writhing and foaming at the mouth. "How long has he been this way?" Jesus asked the father. And he replied, "Since he was very small, and the demon often makes him fall into the fire or into water to kill him. Oh, have mercy on us and do something if you can." "If I can?" Jesus asked. *"Anything* is possible if you have faith." The father instantly replied, "I *do* have faith; oh, help me to have *more!"* When Jesus saw the crowd was growing he rebuked the demon. "O demon of deafness and dumbness," he said, "I command you to come out of this child and enter him no more!" Then the demon screamed terribly and convulsed the boy again and left him; and the boy lay there limp and motionless, to all appearance dead. A murmur ran through the crowd—"He is dead." But Jesus took him by the hand and helped him to his feet and he stood up and was all right!

Afterwards, when Jesus was alone in the house with his disciples, they asked him, "Why couldn't we cast that demon out?" Jesus replied, "Cases like this require prayer."

Leaving that region they traveled through Galilee where he tried to avoid all publicity in order to spend more time with his disciples, teaching them. He would say to them, "I, the Messiah, am going to be betrayed and killed and three days later I will return to life again." But they didn't understand and were afraid to ask him what he meant. And so they arrived at Capernaum. When they were settled in the house where they were to stay he asked them, "What were you discussing out on the road?" But they were ashamed to answer, for they had been arguing about which of them was the greatest! He sat down and called them around him and said, "Anyone wanting to be the greatest must be the least—the servant of all!" Then he placed a little child among them; and taking the child in his arms he said to them, "Anyone who welcomes a little child like this in my name is welcoming me, and anyone who welcomes me is welcoming my Father who sent me!" One of his disciples, John, told him one day, "Teacher, we saw a man using your name to cast out demons; but we told him not to, for he isn't one of our group." "Don't forbid him!" Jesus said. "For no one doing miracles in my name will quickly turn against me. Anyone who isn't against us is for us. If anyone so much as gives you a cup of water because you are Christ's—I say this solemnly—he won't lose his reward. But if someone causes one of these little ones who believe in me to lose faith—it would be better for that man if a huge millstone were tied around his neck and he were thrown into the sea. If your hand does wrong, cut it off. Better live forever with one hand than be thrown into the unquenchable fires of hell with two! If your foot carries you toward evil, cut it off! Better be lame and live forever than have two feet that carry you to hell. And if your eye is sinful, gouge it out. Better enter the Kingdom of God half blind than have two eyes and see the fires of hell, where the worm never dies, and the fire never goes out—where all are salted with fire. Good salt is worthless if it loses its saltiness; it can't season anything. So don't lose your flavor! Live in peace with each other."

Five

Then he left Capernaum and went southward to the Judean borders and into the area east of the Jordan River. And as always there were the crowds; and as usual he taught them.

Some Pharisees came and asked him, "Do you permit divorce?" Of course they were trying to trap him. "What did Moses say about divorce?" Jesus asked them. "He said it was all right," they replied. "He said that all a man has to do is write his wife a letter of dismissal." "And why did he say that?," Jesus asked. "I'll tell you why—it was a concession to your hardhearted wickedness. But it certainly isn't God's way. For from the very first he made man and woman to be joined together permanently in marriage; therefore a man is to leave his father and mother, and he and his wife are united so that they are no longer two, but one. And no man may separate what God has joined together."

Later, when he was alone with his disciples in the house, they brought up the subject again. He told them, "When a man divorces his wife to marry someone else, he commits adultery against her. And if a wife divorces her husband and remarries, she, too, commits adultery."

Once when some mothers were bringing their children to Jesus to bless them, the disciples shooed them away, telling them not to bother him. But when Jesus saw what was happening he was very much displeased with his disciples and said to them, "Let the children come to me, for the Kingdom of God belongs to such as they. Don't send them away! I tell you as seriously as I know how that anyone who refuses to come to God as a little child will never be allowed into his Kingdom." Then he took the children into his arms and placed his hands on their heads and he blessed them.

As he was starting out on a trip, a man came running to him and knelt down and asked, "Good Teacher, what must I do to get to heaven?" "Why do you call me good?," Jesus asked. "Only God is truly good! But as for your question—you know the commandments: don't kill, don't commit adultery, don't steal, don't lie, don't cheat, respect your father and mother." "Teacher," the man replied, "I've never once broken a single one of those laws." Jesus felt genuine love for this man as he looked at him. "You lack only one thing," he told him; "go and sell all you have and give the money to the poor—and you shall have treasure in heaven—and come, follow me." Then the man's face fell, and he went sadly away, for he was very rich. Jesus watched him go, then turned around and said to his disciples, "It's almost impossible for the rich to get into the Kingdom of God!" This amazed them. So Jesus said it again: "Dear children, how hard it is for those who trust in riches to enter the Kingdom of God. It is easier for a camel to go through the eye of a needle than for a rich man to enter the Kingdom of God." The disciples were incredulous! "Then who in the world can be saved, if not a rich man?," they asked. Jesus looked at them intently, then said, "Without God, it is utterly impossible. But with God everything is possible." Then Peter began to mention all that he and the other disciples had left behind. "We've given up everything to follow you," he said. And

Jesus replied, "Let me assure you that no one has ever given up anything—home, brothers, sisters, mother, father, children, or property—for love of me and to tell others the Good News, who won't be given back, a hundred times over, homes, brothers, sisters, mothers, children, and land—with persecutions! All these will be his here on earth, and in the world to come he shall have eternal life. But many people who seem to be important now will be the least important then; and many who are considered least here shall be greatest there."

Now they were on the way to Jerusalem, and Jesus was walking along ahead; and as the disciples were following they were filled with terror and dread. Taking them aside, Jesus once more began describing all that was going to happen to him when they arrived at Jerusalem. "When we get there," he told them, "I, the Messiah, will be arrested and taken before the chief priests and the Jewish leaders, who will sentence me to die and hand me over to the Romans to be killed. They will mock me and spit on me and flog me with their whips and kill me; but after three days I will come back to life again." Then James and John, the sons of Zebedee, came over and spoke to him in a low voice. "Master," they said, "we want you to do us a favor." "What is it?," he asked. "We want to sit on the thrones next to yours in your Kingdom," they said, "one at your right and the other at your left!" But Jesus answered, "You don't know what you are asking! Are you able to drink from the bitter cup of sorrow I must drink from? Or to be baptized with the baptism of suffering I must be baptized with?" "Oh, yes," they said, "we are!" And Jesus said, "You shall indeed drink from my cup and be baptized with my baptism, but I do not have the right to place you on thrones next to mine. Those appointments have already been made." When the other disciples discovered what James and John had asked, they were very indignant. So Jesus called them to him and said, "As you know, the kings and great men of the earth lord it over the people; but among you it is different. Whoever wants to be great among you must be your servant. And whoever wants to be greatest of all must be the slave of all. For even I, the Messiah, am not here to be served, but to help others, and to give my life as a ransom for many."

And so they reached Jericho. Later, as they left town, a great crowd was following. Now it happened that a blind beggar named Bartimaeus (the son of Timaeus) was sitting beside the road as Jesus was going by. When Bartimaeus heard that Jesus from Nazareth was near, he began to shout out, "Jesus, Son of David, have mercy on me!"

"Shut up!" some of the people yelled at him. But he only shouted the louder, again and again, "O Son of David, have mercy on me!" When Jesus heard him, he stopped there in the road and said, "Tell him to come here." So they called the blind man. "You lucky fellow," they said, "come on, he's calling you!" Bartimaeus yanked off his old coat and flung it aside, jumped up and came to Jesus. "What do you want me to do for you?," Jesus asked. "O Teacher," the blind man said, "I want to see!" And Jesus said to him, "All right, it's done. Your faith has healed you." And instantly the blind man could see and followed Jesus down the road!

AS THEY NEARED BETHPHAGE AND BETHANY on the outskirts of Jerusalem and came to the Mount of Olives, Jesus sent two of his disciples on ahead. "Go into that village over there," he told them, "and just as you enter you will see a colt tied up that has never been ridden. Untie him and bring him here. And if anyone asks you what you are doing, just say, 'Our Master needs him and will return him soon.'" Off went the two men and found the colt standing in the street, tied outside a house. As they were untying it, some who were standing there demanded, "What are you doing, untying that colt?" So they said what Jesus had told them to, and then the men agreed.

So the colt was brought to Jesus, and the disciples threw their cloaks across its back for him to ride on. Then many in the crowd spread out their coats along the road before him, while others threw down leafy branches from the fields. He was in the center of the procession with crowds ahead and behind, and all of them shouting, "Hail to the King!" "Praise God for him who comes in the name of the Lord! . . ." "Praise God for the return of our father David's kingdom . . ." "Hail to the King of the universe!" And so he entered Jerusalem and went into the Temple. He looked around carefully at everything and then left—for now it was late in the afternoon—and went out to Bethany with the twelve disciples.

The next morning as they left Bethany, he felt hungry. A little way off he noticed a fig tree in full leaf, so he went over to see if he could find any figs on it. But no, there were only leaves, for it was too early in the season for fruit. Then Jesus said to the tree, "You shall never bear fruit again!" And the disciples heard him say it.

When they arrived back to Jerusalem he went to the Temple and began to drive out the merchants and their customers, and knocked over the tables of the moneychangers and the stalls of those selling doves, and stopped everyone from bringing in loads of merchandise. He told them, "It is written in the Scriptures, 'My Temple is to be a place of prayer for all nations,' but you have turned it into a den of robbers." When the chief priests and other Jewish leaders heard what he had done, they began planning how best to get rid of him. Their problem was their fear of riots because the people were so enthusiastic about Jesus' teaching. That evening as usual they left the city.

The next morning, as the disciples passed the fig tree he had cursed, they saw that it was withered from the roots! Then Peter remembered what Jesus had said to the tree on the previous day and exclaimed, "Look, Teacher! The fig tree you cursed has withered!" In reply Jesus said to the disciples, "If you only have faith in God—this is the absolute truth—you can say to this Mount of Olives, 'Rise up and fall into the Mediterranean,' and your command will be obeyed. All that's required is that you really believe and have no doubt! Listen to me! You can pray for *anything*, and *if you believe, you have it*; it's yours! But when you are praying, first forgive anyone you are holding a grudge against, so that your Father in heaven will forgive you your sins too."

By this time they had arrived in Jerusalem again, and as he was walking through the Temple area, the chief priests and other Jewish leaders came up to him demanding, "What's going on here? Who gave you the authority to drive out the merchants?" Jesus replied, "I'll tell you if you answer one question! What about John the Baptist? Was he sent by God, or not? Answer me!" They talked it over among themselves. "If we reply that God sent him, then he will say, 'All right, why didn't you accept him?' But if we say God didn't send him, then the people will start a riot." (For the people all believed strongly that John was a prophet.) So they said, "We can't answer. We don't know." To which Jesus replied, "Then I won't answer your question either!"

HERE ARE SOME OF THE STORY-ILLUSTRATIONS *Jesus gave to the people at that time:*

"A man planted a vineyard and built a wall around it and dug a pit for pressing out the grape juice, and built a watchman's tower. Then he leased the farm to tenant farmers and moved to another country. At grape-picking time he sent one of his men to collect his share of the crop. But the farmers beat up the man and sent him back empty-handed. The owner then sent another of his men, who received the same treatment, only worse, for his head was seriously injured. The next man he sent was killed; and later, others were either beaten or killed, until there was only one left—his only son. He finally sent him, thinking they would surely give him their full respect. But when the farmers saw him coming they said, 'He will own the farm when his father dies. Come on, let's kill him—and then the farm will be ours!' So they caught him and murdered him and threw his body out of the vineyard. What do you suppose the owner will do when he hears what happened? He will come and kill them all, and lease the vineyard to others. Don't you remember reading this verse in the Scriptures? The Rock the builders threw away became the cornerstone, the most honored stone in the building! This is the Lord's doing and it is an amazing thing to see."

The Jewish leaders wanted to arrest him then and there for using this illustration, for they knew he was pointing at them—they were the wicked farmers in his story. But they were afraid to touch him for fear of a mob. So they left him and went away. But they sent other religious and political leaders to talk with him and try to trap him into saying something he could be arrested for. "Teacher," these spies said, "we know you tell the truth no matter what! You aren't influenced by the opinions and desires of men, but sincerely teach the ways of God. Now tell us, is it right to pay taxes to Rome, or not?" Jesus saw their trick and said, "Show me a coin and I'll tell you." When they handed it to him he asked, "Whose picture and title is this on the coin?" They replied, "The emperor's." "All right," he said, "if it is his, give it to him. But everything that belongs to God must be given to God!" And they scratched their heads in bafflement at his reply. Then the Sadducees stepped forward—a group of men who say there is no resurrection. Here was their question: "Teacher, Moses gave us a law that when a man dies without children, the man's brother should marry his widow and have children in his brother's name. Well, there were seven brothers and the oldest married and died, and left no children. So the second brother married the widow, but soon he died too and left no children. Then the next brother married her and died without children, and so on until all were dead, and still there were no children; and last of all, the woman died too. What we want to know is this: In the resurrection, whose wife will she be, for she had been the wife of each of them?" Jesus replied, "Your trouble is that you don't know the Scriptures and don't know the power of God. For when these seven brothers and the woman rise from the dead, they won't be married—they will be like the angels. But now as to whether there will be a resurrection—have you never read in the book of Exodus about Moses and the burning bush? God said to Moses, 'I am the God of Abraham, and I *am* the God of Isaac, and I *am* the God of Jacob.' God was telling Moses that these men, though dead for hundreds of years, were still very much alive, for he would not have said, 'I am the God' of those who don't exist! You have made a serious error."

One of the teachers of religion who was standing there listening to the discussion realized that Jesus had answered well. So he asked, "Of all the commandments, which is the most important?" Jesus replied, "The one that says, 'Hear, O Israel! The Lord our God is the one and only God. And you must love him with all your heart and soul and mind and strength.' The second is: 'You must love others as much as yourself.' No other commandments are greater than these." The teacher of religion replied, "Sir, you have spoken a true word in saying that there is only one God and no other. And I know it is far more important to love him with all my heart and understanding and strength, and to love others as myself, than to offer all kinds of sacrifices on the altar of the Temple." Realizing this man's understanding, Jesus said to him, "You are not far from the Kingdom of God." And after that, no one dared ask him any more questions.

Later, as Jesus was teaching the people in the Temple area, he asked them this question: "Why do your religious teachers claim that the Messiah must be a descendant of King David? For David himself said—and the Holy Spirit was speaking through him when he said it—'God said to my Lord, sit at my right hand until I make your enemies your footstool.' Since David called him his Lord, how can he be his *son?*" (This sort of reasoning delighted the crowd and they listened to him with great interest.) Here are some of the other things he taught them at this time: "Beware of the teachers of religion! For they love to wear the robes of the rich and scholarly, and to have everyone bow to them as they walk through the markets. They love to sit in the best seats in the synagogues and at the places of honor at banquets—but they shamelessly cheat widows out of their homes and then, to cover up the kind of men they really are, they pretend to be pious by praying long prayers in public. Because of this, their punishment will be the greater." Then he went over to the collection boxes in the Temple and sat and watched as the crowds dropped in their money. Some who were rich put in large amounts. Then a poor widow came and dropped in two pennies. He called his disciples to him and remarked, "That poor widow has given more than all those rich men put together! For they gave a little of their extra fat, while she gave up her last penny."

Six

Okay, let's move on to Luke's gospel.

Luke, by the way, was the author of the third Gospel, the other three by Matthew, Mark and John, each of them Jews. Luke, however, was a Gentile and is still regarded as the best historian of the first century. And some scholars believe that it was Luke who interviewed Mary—who would have been in her eighties or nineties—in order to capture the fascinating detail surrounding Jesus' birth.

So, let's see what Luke has to say.

In as much as many have undertaken to draw up an account of the things that have been fulfilled among us, just as they were handed down to us by those who from the first were eyewitnesses and servants of the word. Therefore, since I myself have carefully investigated everything from the beginning, it seemed good also to me to write an orderly account for you, most excellent Theophilus, so that you may know the certainty of the things you have been taught. In the time of Herod king of Judea there was a priest named Zechariah, who belonged to the priestly division of

Abijah; his wife Elizabeth was also a descendant of Aaron. Both of them were upright in the sight of God, observing all the Lord's commandments and regulations blamelessly, but they had no children, because Elizabeth was barren; and they were both well along in years.

Once when Zechariah's division was on duty and he was serving as priest before God, he was chosen by lot, according to the custom of the priesthood, to go into the temple of the Lord and burn incense. And when the time for the burning of incense came, all the assembled worshipers were praying outside. Then an angel of the Lord appeared to him, standing at the right side of the altar of incense. When Zechariah saw Him, he was startled and was gripped with fear. But the angel said to Him: "Do not be afraid, Zechariah; your prayer has been heard. Your wife Elizabeth will bear you a son, and you are to give Him the name John. He will be a joy and delight to you, and many will rejoice because of his birth, for he will be great in the sight of the Lord. He is never to take wine or other fermented drink, and he will be filled with the Holy Spirit even from birth. Many of the people of Israel will he bring back to the Lord their God. And he will go on before the Lord, in the spirit and power of Elijah, to turn the hearts of the fathers to their children and the disobedient to the wisdom of the righteous—to make ready a people prepared for the Lord."

Zechariah asked the angel, "How can I be sure of this? I am an old man and my wife is well along in years." The angel answered, "I am Gabriel. I stand in the presence of God, and I have been sent to speak to you and to tell you this good news. And now you will be silent and not able to speak until the day this happens, because you did not believe my words, which will come true at their proper time." Meanwhile, the people were waiting for Zechariah and wondering why he stayed so long in the temple. When he came out, he could not speak to them. They realized he had seen a vision in the temple, for he kept making signs to them but remained unable to speak.

When his time of service was completed, he returned home. After this his wife Elizabeth became pregnant and for five months remained in seclusion. "The Lord has done this for me," she said. "In these days he has shown his favor and taken away my disgrace among the people." In the sixth month, God sent the angel Gabriel to Nazareth, a town in Galilee, to a virgin pledged to be married to a man named Joseph, a descendant of David. The virgin's name was Mary. The angel went to her and said, "Greetings, you who are highly favored! The Lord is with you." Mary was greatly troubled at his words and wondered what kind of greeting this might be. But the angel said to her, "Do not be afraid, Mary, you have found favor with God. You will be with child and give birth to a son, and you are to give Him the name Jesus. He will be great and will be called the Son of the Most High. The Lord God will give Him the throne of his father David, and he will reign over the house of Jacob forever; his kingdom will never end." "How will this be," Mary asked the angel, "since I am a virgin?" The angel answered, "The Holy Spirit will come upon you, and the power of the Most High will overshadow you. So the holy one to be born will be called the Son of God. Even Elizabeth your relative is going to have a child in her old age, and she who was said to be barren is in her sixth month. For nothing is impossible with God." "I am the Lord's servant," Mary answered. "May it be to me as you have said." Then the angel left her.

At that time Mary got ready and hurried to a town in the hill country of Judea, where she entered Zechariah's home and greeted Elizabeth. When Elizabeth heard Mary's greeting, the baby leaped in her womb, and Elizabeth was filled with the Holy Spirit. In a loud voice she exclaimed: "Blessed are you among women, and blessed is the child you will bear! But why am I so favored, that the mother of my Lord should come to me? As soon as the sound of your greeting reached my ears, the baby in my womb leaped for joy. Blessed is she who has believed that what the Lord has said to her will be accomplished!" And Mary said: "My soul glorifies the Lord and my spirit rejoices in God my Savior, for he has been mindful of the humble state of his servant. From now on all generations will call me blessed, for the Mighty One has done great things for me—holy is his name. His mercy extends to those who fear Him, from generation to generation. He has performed mighty deeds with his arm; he has scattered those who are proud in their inmost thoughts. He has brought down rulers from their thrones but has lifted up the humble. He has filled the hungry with good things but has sent the rich away empty. He has helped his servant Israel, remembering to be merciful to Abraham and his descendants forever, even as he said to our fathers."

Mary stayed with Elizabeth for about three months and then returned home. When it was time for Elizabeth to have her baby, she gave birth to a son. Her neighbors and relatives heard that the Lord had shown her great mercy, and they shared her joy. On the eighth day they came to circumcise the child, and they were going to name Him after his father Zechariah, but his mother spoke up and said, "No! He is to be called John." They said to her, "There is no one among your relatives who has that name." Then they made signs to his father, to find out what he would like to name the child. He asked for a writing tablet, and to everyone's astonishment he wrote, "His name is John." Immediately his mouth was opened and his tongue was loosed, and he began to speak, praising God. The neighbors were all filled with awe, and throughout the hill country of Judea people were talking about all these things. Everyone who heard this wondered about it, asking, "What then is this child going to be?" For the Lord's hand was with Him. His father Zechariah was filled with the Holy Spirit and prophesied: "Praise be to the

Lord, the God of Israel, because he has come and has redeemed his people. He has raised up a horn of salvation for us in the house of his servant David as he said through his holy prophets of long ago, salvation from our enemies and from the hand of all who hate us, to show mercy to our fathers and to remember his holy covenant, the oath he swore to our father Abraham: to rescue us from the hand of our enemies, and to enable us to serve Him without fear, in holiness and righteousness before Him all our days. And you, my child, will be called a prophet of the Most High; for you will go on before the Lord to prepare the way for Him, to give his people the knowledge of salvation through the forgiveness of their sins, because of the tender mercy of our God, by which the rising sun will come to us from heaven to shine on those living in darkness and in the shadow of death, to guide our feet into the path of peace."

And the child grew and became strong in spirit; and he lived in the desert until he appeared publicly to Israel.

Seven

Now it came about in those days that a decree went out from Caesar Augustus, that a census be taken of all the inhabited earth. This was the first census taken while Quirinius was governor of Syria. And all were proceeding to register for the census, everyone to his own city. And Joseph also went up from Galilee, from the city of Nazareth, to Judea, to the city of David, which is called Bethlehem, because he was of the house and family of David, in order to register, along with Mary, who was engaged to Him, and was with child. And it came about that while they were there, the days were completed for her to give birth. And she gave birth to her first-born son; and she wrapped Him in cloths, and laid Him in a manger, because there was no room for them in the inn. And in the same region there were some shepherds staying out in the fields, and keeping watch over their flock by night. And an angel of the Lord suddenly stood before them, and the glory of the Lord shone around them; and they were terribly frightened. And the angel said to them, "Do not be afraid; for behold, I bring you good news of a great joy which shall be for all the people; for today in the city of David there has been born for you a Savior, who is Christ the Lord. And this will be a sign for you: you will find a baby wrapped in cloths, and lying in a manger."

And suddenly there appeared with the angel a multitude of the heavenly host praising God, and saying, "Glory to God in the highest, And on earth peace among men with whom He is pleased." And it came about when the angels had gone away from them into heaven, that the shepherds were saying to one another, "Let us go straight to Bethlehem then, and see this thing that has happened which the Lord has made known to us." And they came in haste and found their way to Mary and Joseph, and the baby as He lay in the manger. And when they had seen this, they made known the statement which had been told them about this Child. And all who heard it wondered at the things which were told them by the shepherds.

But Mary treasured up all these things, pondering them in her heart. And the shepherds went back, glorifying and praising God for all that they had heard and seen, just as had been told them. And when eight days were completed before His circumcision, His name was called Jesus, the name given by the angel before He was conceived in the womb. And when the days for their purification according to the law of Moses were completed, they brought Him up to Jerusalem to present Him to the Lord as it is written in the Law of the Lord, "EVERY *first-born* MALE THAT OPENS THE WOMB SHALL BE CALLED HOLY TO THE LORD," and to offer a sacrifice according to what was said in the Law of the Lord, "A PAIR OF TURTLEDOVES, OR TWO YOUNG PIGEONS."

And behold, there was a man in Jerusalem whose name was Simeon; and this man was righteous and devout, looking for the consolation of Israel; and the Holy Spirit was upon Him. And it had been revealed to Him by the Holy Spirit that he would not see death before he had seen the Lord's Christ. And he came in the Spirit into the temple; and when the parents brought in the child Jesus, to carry out for Him the custom of the Law, then he took Him into his arms, and blessed God, and said, "Now Lord, You will let Your bond-servant depart In peace, according to Your word; For my eyes have seen Your salvation, which Thou hast prepared in the presence of all peoples, A LIGHT OF REVELATION TO THE GENTILES, And the glory of Your people Israel." And His father and mother were amazed at the things which were being said about Him. And Simeon blessed them, and said to Mary His mother, "Behold, this Child is appointed for the fall and rise of many in Israel, and for a sign to be opposed, and a sword will pierce even your own soul—to the end that thoughts from many hearts may be revealed."

And there was a prophetess, Anna the daughter of Phanuel, of the tribe of Asher. She was advanced in years, having lived with a husband seven years after her marriage, and then as a widow to the age of eighty-four. And she never left the temple, serving night and day with fastings and prayers. And at that very moment she came up and began giving thanks to God, and continued to speak of Him to all those who were looking for the redemption of Jerusalem. And when they had performed everything according to the Law of the Lord, they returned to Galilee, to their own city of Nazareth.

And the Child continued to grow and become strong, increasing in wisdom; and the grace of God was upon Him. And His parents used to go to Jerusalem every year at the Feast of the Passover. And when He became twelve, they went up there according to the custom of the Feast; and as they were returning, after spending the full number of days, the boy Jesus stayed behind in Jerusalem. And His parents were unaware of it, but supposed Him to be in the caravan, and went a day's journey; and they began looking for Him among their relatives and acquaintances. And when they did not find Him, they returned to Jerusalem, looking for Him. And it came about that after three days they found Him in the temple, sitting in the midst of the teachers, both listening to them, and asking them questions. And all who heard Him were amazed at His understanding and His answers. And when they saw Him, they were astonished; and His mother said to Him, "Son, why have You treated us this way? Behold, Your father and I have been anxiously looking for You." And He said to them, "Why is it that you were looking for Me? Did you not know that I had to be in My Father's house?" And they did not understand the statement which He had made to them. And He went down with them, and came to Nazareth; and He continued in subjection to them; and His mother treasured all these things in her heart. And Jesus kept increasing in wisdom and stature, and in favor with God and men.

Eight

Now in the fifteenth year of the reign of Tiberius Caesar, when Pontius Pilate was governor of Judea, and Herod was tetrarch of Galilee, and his brother Philip was tetrarch of the region of Ituraea and Trachonitis, and Lysanias was tetrarch of Abilene, in the high priesthood of Annas and Caiaphas, the word of God came to John, the son of Zacharias, in the wilderness. And he came into all the district around the Jordan, preaching a baptism of repentance for the forgiveness of sins; as it is written in the book of the words of Isaiah the prophet, "THE VOICE OF ONE CRYING IN THE WILDERNESS, 'MAKE READY THE WAY OF THE LORD, MAKE HIS PATHS STRAIGHT. EVERY RAVINE SHALL BE FILLED UP, AND EVERY MOUNTAIN AND HILL SHALL BE BROUGHT LOW; AND THE CROOKED SHALL BECOME STRAIGHT, AND THE ROUGH ROADS SMOOTH; AND ALL FLESH SHALL SEE THE SALVATION OF GOD.'"

He therefore began saying to the multitudes who were going out to be baptized by Him, "You brood of vipers, who warned you to flee from the wrath to come? Therefore bring forth fruits in keeping with repentance, and do not begin to say to yourselves, 'We have Abraham for our father,' for I say to you that God is able from these stones to raise up children to Abraham. And also the axe is already laid at the root of the trees; every tree therefore that does not bear good fruit is cut down and thrown into the fire."

And the multitudes were questioning Him, saying, "Then what shall we do?" And he would answer and say to them, "Let the man who has two tunics share with Him who has none; and let Him who has food do likewise." And some tax-gatherers also came to be baptized, and they said to Him, "Teacher, what shall we do?" And he said to them, "Collect no more than what you have been ordered to." And some soldiers were questioning Him, saying, "And what about us, what shall we do?" And he said to them, "Do not take money from anyone by force, or accuse anyone falsely, and be content with your wages."

Now while the people were in a state of expectation and all were wondering in their hearts about John, as to whether he might be the Christ, John answered and said to them all, "As for me, I baptize you with water; but One is coming who is mightier than I, and I am not fit to untie the thong of His sandals; He will baptize you with the Holy Spirit and fire. And His winnowing fork is in His hand to thoroughly clear His threshing floor, and to gather the wheat into His barn; but He will burn up the chaff with unquenchable fire."

So with many other exhortations also he preached the gospel to the people. But when Herod the tetrarch was reproved by Him on account of Herodias, his brother's wife, and on account of all the wicked things which Herod had done, he added this also to them all, that he locked John up in prison.

Now it came about when all the people were baptized, that Jesus also was baptized, and while He was praying, heaven was opened, and the Holy Spirit descended upon Him in bodily form like a dove, and a voice came out of heaven, "Thou art My beloved Son, in Thee I am well-pleased."

And when He began His ministry, Jesus Himself was about thirty years of age, being supposedly the *son* of Joseph, the *son* of Eli, the *son* of Matthat, the *son* of Levi, the *son* of Melchi, the *son* of Jannai, the *son* of Joseph, the *son* of Mattathias, the *son* of Amos, the *son* of Nahum, the *son* of Hesli, the *son* of Naggai, the *son* of Maath, the *son* of Mattathias, the *son* of Semein, the *son* of Josech, the *son* of Joda, the *son* of Joanan, the *son* of Rhesa, the *son* of Zerubbabel, the *son* of Shealtiel, the *son* of Neri, the *son* of Melchi, the *son* of Addi, the *son* of Cosam, the *son* of Elmadam, the *son* of Er, the *son* of Joshua, the *son* of Eliezer, the son of Jorim, the *son* of Matthat, the *son* of Levi, the *son* of Simeon, the *son* of Judah, the *son* of Joseph, the *son* of Jonam, the *son* of Eliakim the *son* of Melea, the *son* of Menna, the *son* of Mattatha, the *son* of Nathan, the *son* of David, the *son* of Jesse, the *son* of Obed, the *son* of Boaz, the *son* of Salmon, the *son* of Nahshon, the *son* of Amminadab, the *son* of Admin, the *son* of Ram, the *son* of Hezron, the *son* of Perez, the *son* of Judah, the *son* of Jacob, the *son* of Isaac, the *son* of Abraham, the *son* of Terah, the *son* of Nahor the *son* of Serug, the *son* of Reu, the *son* of Peleg, the *son* of Heber, the *son* of Shelah, the *son* of Cainan, the *son* of Arphaxad, the *son* of Shem, the *son* of Noah, the *son* of Lamech, the *son* of Methuselah, the *son* of Enoch, the *son* of Jared, the *son* of Mahalaleel, the *son* of Cainan, the *son* of Enosh, the *son* of Seth, the *son* of Adam, the *son* of God.

NINE

*B*EFORE WE GO FURTHER, A FEW *words about Matthew's gospel. Readers need not be reminded that in first century Palestine there was no television, no nightly news re-caps on the radio, no Internet, and no DVDs. The printing press was 500 years into the future. Those few who could read might be fortunate enough to have access to those few pieces of parchment that bore some semblance of "news." But for the most part, "news" traveled by word of mouth. Although Jesus and a few others spoke Aramaic, the Lingua Franca of the day was Greek, both spoken and written. And Matthew was well aware of this, he the unpopular man who collected taxes for the hated Roman occupiers. And he knew that his readers felt the same way. That is why Matthew begins his gospel with the genealogy that goes all the way from Adam to Jesus' birth in Bethlehem, as witnessed by the traveling Maji. So, let's read it:*

The book of the genealogy of Jesus Christ, the son of David, the son of Abraham. Abraham became the father of Isaac, Isaac the father of Jacob, Jacob the father of Judah and his brothers. Judah became the father of Perez and Zerah, whose mother was

Tamar. Perez became the father of Hezron, Hezron the father of Ram, Ram the father of Amminadab. Amminadab became the father of Nahshon, Nahshon the father of Salmon, Salmon the father of Boaz, whose mother was Rahab. Boaz became the father of Obed, whose mother was Ruth. Obed became the father of Jesse, Jesse the father of David the king. David became the father of Solomon, whose mother had been the wife of Uriah. Solomon became the father of Rehoboam, Rehoboam the father of Abijah, Abijah the father of Asaph. Asaph became the father of Jehoshaphat, Jehoshaphat the father of Joram, Joram the father of Uzziah. Uzziah became the father of Jotham, Jotham the father of Ahaz, Ahaz the father of Hezekiah. Hezekiah became the father of Manasseh, Manasseh the father of Amos, Amos the father of Josiah. Josiah became the father of Jeconiah and his brothers at the time of the Babylonian exile.

After the Babylonian exile, Jechoniah became the father of Shealtiel, Shealtiel the father of Zerubbabel, Zerubbabel the father of Abiud. Abiud became the father of Eliakim, Eliakim the father of Azor, Azor the father of Zadok. Zadok became the father of Achim, Achim the father of Eliud, Eliud the father of Eleazar. Eleazar became the father of Matthan, Matthan the father of Jacob, Jacob the father of Joseph, the husband of Mary. Of her was born Jesus who is called the Messiah.

Thus the total number of generations from Abraham to David is fourteen generations; from David to the Babylonian exile, fourteen generations; from the Babylonian exile to the Messiah, fourteen generations.

NOW THIS IS HOW THE BIRTH of Jesus Christ came about. When his mother Mary was betrothed to Joseph, but before they lived together, she was found with child through the holy Spirit. Joseph her husband, since he was a righteous man, willing to expose her to shame, decided to divorce her quietly.

Such was his intention when, behold, the angel of the Lord appeared to him in a dream and said, "Joseph, son of David, do not be afraid to take Mary your wife into your home. For it is through the holy Spirit that this child has been conceived in her. She will bear a son and you are to name him Jesus, because he will save his people from their sins."

All this took place to fulfill what the Lord had said through the prophet: "Behold, the virgin shall be with child and bear a son, and they shall name him Emmanuel," which means "God is with us." When Joseph awoke, he did as the angel of the Lord had commanded him and took his wife into his home. He had no relations with her until she bore a son.

AND JESUS, FULL OF THE HOLY SPIRIT, returned from the Jordan and was led about by the Spirit in the wilderness for forty days, being tempted by the devil. And He ate nothing during those days; and when they had ended, He became hungry. And the devil said to Him, "If You are the Son of God, tell this stone to become bread." And Jesus answered Him, "It is written, 'MAN SHALL NOT LIVE ON BREAD ALONE.'" And he led Him up and showed Him all the kingdoms of the world in a moment of time. And the devil said to Him, "I will give You all this domain and its glory; for it has been handed over to me, and I give it to whomever I wish. Therefore if You worship before me, it shall all be Yours." And Jesus answered and said to Him, "It is written, 'YOU SHALL WORSHIP THE LORD YOUR GOD AND SERVE HIM ONLY.'"

And he led Him to Jerusalem and had Him stand on the pinnacle of the temple, and said to Him, "If You are the Son of God, throw Yourself down from here; for it is written, 'HE WILL GIVE HIS ANGELS CHARGE CONCERNING YOU TO GUARD YOU,' and, 'ON their HANDS THEY WILL BEAR YOU UP, LEST YOU STRIKE YOUR FOOT AGAINST A STONE.'"

And Jesus answered and said to Him, "It is said, 'YOU SHALL NOT PUT THE LORD YOUR GOD TO THE TEST.'" And when the devil had finished every temptation, he departed from Him until an opportune time. And Jesus returned to Galilee in the power of the Spirit; and news about Him spread through all the surrounding district. And He began teaching in their synagogues and was praised by all. And He came to Nazareth, where He had been brought up; and as was His custom, He entered the synagogue on the Sabbath, and stood up to read.

And the book of the prophet Isaiah was handed to Him. And He opened the book, and found the place where it was written, "THE SPIRIT OF THE LORD IS UPON ME, BECAUSE HE ANOINTED ME TO PREACH THE GOSPEL TO THE POOR. HE HAS SENT ME TO PROCLAIM RELEASE TO THE CAPTIVES, AND RECOVERY OF SIGHT TO THE BLIND, TO SET FREE THOSE WHO ARE DOWNTRODDEN, TO PROCLAIM THE FAVORABLE YOUAR OF THE LORD." And He closed the book, and gave it back to the attendant, and sat down; and the eyes of all in the synagogue were fixed upon Him. And He began to say to them, "Today this Scripture has been fulfilled in your hearing." And all were speaking well of Him, and wondering at the gracious words which were falling from His lips; and they were saying, "Is this not Joseph's son?" And He said to them, "No doubt you will quote this proverb to Me, 'Physician, heal yourself! Whatever we heard was done at Capernaum, do here in your home town as well.'" And He said, "Truly I say to you, no prophet is welcome in his home town. But I say to you in truth, there were many widows in Israel in the days of Elijah, when the sky was shut up for three years and six months, when a great famine came over all the land; and young Elijah was sent to none of them, but only to Zarephath, in the land of Sidon, to a woman who was a widow. And there were many lepers in Israel in the time of Elisha the prophet; and none of them was cleansed, but only Naaman the Syrian." And all in the synagogue were filled with rage as they heard these things; and they rose up and cast Him out of the city, and led Him to the brow of the hill on which their city had been built, in order to throw Him down the cliff. But passing through their midst, He went His way. And He came down to Capernaum, a city of Galilee. And He was teaching them on the Sabbath; and they were amazed at His teaching, for His message was with authority.

And there was a man in the synagogue possessed by the spirit of an unclean demon, and he cried out with a loud voice, "Ha! What do we have to do with You, Jesus of Nazareth? Have You come to destroy us? I know who You are—the Holy One of God!" And Jesus rebuked Him, saying, "Be quiet and come out of Him!" And when the demon had thrown Him down in their midst, he came out of Him without doing Him any harm. And amazement came upon them all, and they began discussing with one another saying, "What is this message? For with authority and power He commands the unclean spirits, and they come out."

And the report about Him was getting out into every locality in the surrounding district. And He arose and left the synagogue, and entered Simon's home. Now Simon's mother-in-law was suffering from a high fever; and they made request of Him on her behalf. And standing over her, He rebuked the fever, and it left her; and she immediately arose and waited on them. And while the sun was setting, all who had any sick with various diseases brought them to Him; and laying His hands on every one of them, He was healing them. And demons also were coming out of many, crying out and saying, "You are the Son of God!" And rebuking them, He would not allow them to speak, because they knew Him to be the Christ.

And when day came, He departed and went to a lonely place; and the multitudes were searching for Him, and came to Him, and tried to keep Him from going. But He said to them, "I must preach the kingdom of God to the other cities also, for I was sent for this purpose." And He kept on preaching in the synagogues of Judea.

Now it came about that while the multitude were pressing around Him and listening to the word of God, He was standing by the lake of Gennesaret; and He saw two boats lying at the edge of the lake; but the fishermen had gotten out of them, and were washing their nets. And He got into one of the boats, which was Simon's, and asked Him to put out a little way from the land. And He sat down and began teaching the multitudes from the boat. And when He had finished speaking, He said to Simon, "Put out into the deep water and let down your nets for a catch." And Simon answered and said, "Master, we worked hard all night and caught nothing, but at Your bidding I will let down the nets." And when they had done this, they enclosed a great quantity of fish; and their nets began to break; and they signaled to their partners in the other boat, for them to come and help them. And they came, and filled both of the boats, so that they began to sink. But when Simon Peter saw that, he fell down at Jesus' feet, saying, "Depart from me, for I am a sinful man, O Lord!" For amazement had seized Him and all his companions because of the catch of fish which they had taken; and so also James and John, sons of Zebedee, who were partners with Simon. And Jesus said to Simon, "Do not fear, from now on you will be catching men." And when they had brought their boats to land, they left everything and followed Him.

And it came about that while He was in one of the cities, behold, there was a man full of leprosy; and when he saw Jesus, he fell on his face and implored Him, saying, "Lord, if You are willing, You can make me clean." And He stretched out His hand, and touched Him, saying, "I am willing; be cleansed." And immediately the leprosy left him. And He ordered him to tell no one, "But go and show yourself to the priest, and make an offering for your cleansing, just as Moses commanded, for a testimony to them." But the news about Him was spreading even farther, and great multitudes were gathering to hear Him and to be healed of their sicknesses. But He Himself would often slip away to the wilderness and pray.

And it came about one day that He was teaching; and there were some Pharisees and teachers of the law sitting there, who had come from every village of Galilee and Judea and from Jerusalem; and the power of the Lord was present for Him to perform healing. And behold, some men were carrying on a bed a man who was paralyzed; and they were trying to bring him in, and to set him down in front of Him. And not finding any way to bring him in because of the crowd, they went up on the roof and let him down through the tiles with his stretcher, right in the center, in front of Jesus. And seeing their faith, He said, "Friend, your sins are forgiven you." And the scribes and the Pharisees began to reason, saying, "Who is this man who speaks blasphemies? Who can forgive sins, but God alone?" But Jesus, aware of their reasonings, answered and said to them, "Why are you reasoning in your hearts? Which is easier, to say, 'Your sins have been forgiven you,' or to say, 'Rise and walk'? But in order that you may know that the Son of Man has authority on earth to forgive sins,"—He said to the paralytic: "I say to you, rise, and take up your stretcher and go home." And at once he rose up before them, and took up what he had been lying on, and went home, glorifying God. And they were all seized with astonishment and began glorifying God; and they were filled with fear, saying, "We have seen remarkable things today."

And after that He went out, and noticed a tax-gatherer named Levi, sitting in the tax office, and He said to him, "Follow Me." And he left everything behind, and rose and began to follow Him. And Levi gave a big reception for Him in his house; and there was a great crowd of tax-gatherers and other people who were reclining at the table with them. And the Pharisees and their scribes began grumbling at His disciples, saying, "Why do you eat and drink with the tax-gatherers and sinners?" And Jesus answered and said to them, "It is not those who are well who need a physician, but those who are sick. I have not come to call the righteous but sinners to repentance." And they said to Him, "The disciples of John often fast and offer prayers; the disciples of the Pharisees also do the same; but Yours eat and drink." And Jesus said to them, "You cannot make the attendants of the bridegroom fast while the bridegroom is with them, can you? But the days will come; and when the bridegroom is taken away from them, then they will fast in those days."

And He was also telling them a parable: "No one tears a piece from a new garment and puts it on an old garment; otherwise he will both tear the new, and the piece from the new will not match the old. And no one puts new wine into old wineskins; otherwise the new wine will burst the skins, and it will be spilled out, and the skins will be ruined. But new wine must be put into fresh wineskins. And no one, after drinking old wine wishes for new; for he says, 'The old is good enough.'"

Ten

And Jesus, full of the Holy Spirit, returned from the Jordan, and was led in the Spirit in the wilderness during forty days, being tempted of the devil. And He did eat nothing in those days: and when they were completed, He hungered. And the devil said unto Him, "if thou art the Son of God, command this stone that it become bread." And Jesus answered unto him, "It is written, 'Man shall not live by bread alone.'"

And he led Him up, and showed Him all the kingdoms of the world in a moment of time. And the devil said unto Him, "To thee will I give all this authority, and the glory of them: for it has been delivered unto me; and to whomsoever I will I give it. If You therefore will worship before me, it shall all be Yours." And Jesus answered and said unto Him, "It is written, 'you shall worship the Lord your God, and Him only shall you serve.'" And he led Him to Jerusalem, and set Him on the pinnacle of the temple, and said unto Him, "If you are the Son of God, cast yourself down from here: for it is written, 'He shall give his angels charge concerning thee, to guard thee:' and, 'On their hands they shall bear thee up, lest You dash your foot against a stone.'" And Jesus answering said unto him, "It is said, 'you shall not make trial of the Lord your God.'" And when the devil had completed every temptation, he departed from Him for a season. And Jesus returned in the power of the Spirit into Galilee: and fame went out concerning Him through all the region round about.

And He taught in their synagogues, being glorified by all. And He came to Nazareth, where He had been brought up: and He entered, as his custom was, into the synagogue on the sabbath day, and stood up to read. And there was delivered unto Him the book of the prophet Isaiah. And He opened the book, and found the place where it was written, "The Spirit of the Lord is upon Me, Because he anointed me to preach good tidings to the poor: He has sent me to proclaim release to the captives, And recovering of sight to the blind, To set at liberty them that are bruised, To proclaim the acceptable year of the Lord." And He closed the book, and gave it back to the attendant, and sat down: and the eyes of all in the synagogue were fastened on Him. And he began to say unto them, "Today has this scripture been fulfilled in your presence."

And all bore Him witness, and wondered at the words of grace which proceeded out of His mouth: and they said, "Is not this Joseph's son?" And He said to them, "Doubtless you will say unto Me this parable, Physician, heal yourself: whatsoever we have heard done at Capernaum, do also here in your own country." And he said, "Verily I say unto you, No prophet is acceptable in his own country. But of a truth I say unto you, There were many widows in Israel in the days of Elijah, when the heaven was shut up three years and six months, when there came a great famine over all the land; and unto none of them was Elijah sent, but only to Zarephath, in the land of Sidon, unto a woman that was a widow. And there were many lepers in Israel in the time of Elisha the prophet; and none of them was cleansed, but only Naaman the Syrian."

And they were all filled with wrath in the synagogue, as they heard these things and they rose up, and cast Him forth out of the city, and led Him unto the brow of the hill whereon their city was built, that they might throw Him down headlong. But He passed through the midst of them and went His way. And he came down to Capernaum, a city of Galilee. And He was teaching them on the sabbath day: and they were astonished at His teaching; for His word was with authority. And in the synagogue there was a man, that had a spirit of an unclean demon; and he cried out with a loud voice, "Ah! what have we to do with You, Jesus of Nazarene? Have You come to destroy us? I know who You are, the Holy One of God."

And Jesus rebuked him, saying, "Hold your peace, and come out of him." And when the demon had thrown him down in the midst, he came out of him, having done him no harm. And amazement came upon all, and they spoke together, one with another, saying, "What is this word? for with authority and power He commands the unclean spirits, and they come out."

And there went forth a rumor concerning Him into every place of the region. And he rose up from the synagogue, and entered into the house of Simon. And Simon's wife's mother was suffering with a great fever; and they begged Him for her. And He stood over her, and rebuked the fever; and it left her: and immediately she rose up and ministered to them. And when the sun was setting, all they that had any sick with divers diseases brought them unto Him; and he laid His hands on every one of them, and healed them. And demons also came out from many, crying out, and saying, "Thou art the Son of God." And rebuking them, He ordered them not to speak, because they knew that He was the Christ.

And when it was day, He came out and went into a desert place: and the multitudes sought after Him, and came unto Him, and would have stayed with Him, that he should not go from them. But He said unto them, "I must preach the good tidings of the kingdom of God to the other cities also: for therefore was I sent." And He was preaching in the synagogues of Galilee.

Eleven

After these things Jesus and His disciples came into the land of Judea and there He was spending time with them and baptizing. And John also was baptizing in Aenon near Salim because there was much water there and they were coming and being baptized. For John had not yet been thrown into prison. There arose a discussion on the part of John's disciples with a Jew about purification. And they came to John and said to him, "Rabbi, He who was with you beyond the Jordan, to whom you have borne witness, behold He is baptizing and all are coming to Him." John answered and said, "A man can receive nothing unless it has been given Him from heaven. Your yourselves bear me witness, that I said, 'I am not the Christ but I have been sent before.'"

But when Herod the tetrarch was reproved by him on account of Herodias, his brother's wife, and on account of the wicked things which Herod done, he added this also to them all, that he locked John up in prison.

Luke's brief account of the Baptizer's jailing suggests that John had been a thorn in Herod's side for some time. It's helpful to understand a bit more about this relationship. At an earlier time, Herodias had been the wife of Herod's half-brother, Philip, her uncle, so that her marriage to Herod was an incestuous relationship. John knew about this, didn't like it, and had the courage to say so to anyone who would listen. Little wonder that Herod locked Him up, to keep him quiet!

And King Herod heard of it, for his name had become well known, and people were saying, "John the Baptist has risen from the dead and that is why these miraculous powers are at work in Him." But others were saying, "He is Elijah," and others were saying, "He is a prophet, like the prophets of old." But when Herod heard of it he kept saying, "John, whom I beheaded, has risen!" For Herod himself had sent and had John arrested and bound in prison on account of Herodias, the wife of his brother Philip, because he had married her. And immediately she came in haste before the king and asked, saying, "I want you to give me right away the head of John the Baptist on a platter." And although the king was very sorry, because of his oaths and because of his dinner guests, he was unwilling to refuse her. And immediately the king sent an executioner and commanded Him to bring back his head. And he went and had him beheaded in the prison, and brought the head on a platter, and gave it to the girl, and the girl gave it to her mother. And when the disciples heard about this, they came and took away the body and laid it in a tomb.

After these things there was a feast of the Jews and Jesus went up to Jerusalem. Now there is in Jerusalem by the sheep gate a pool, which in Hebrew is called Bethesda, having five porticoes. In these lay a multitude of those who were sick, lame, blind and withered, waiting for the moving of the waters, for an angel of the Lord went down at certain seasons into the pool, and stirred up the water, whoever then first, after the stirring of the water, stepped in was made well from whatever disease with which he was afflicted. And a certain man was there who had been thirty eight years in his sickness. When Jesus saw him lying there, and knew that he had already been a long time in that condition, He said to him, "Do you wish to get well?" The sick man answered Him, "Sir, I have no man to put me into the pool when the water is stirred up, but while I am coming, another steps in before me." Jesus said to Him, "Arise, take up your pallet and walk." And immediately the man became well and took up his pallet and began to walk. Now it was the Sabbath on that day. Therefore the Jews were saying to him who was cured, "It is the Sabbath and it is not permissible for you to carry your pallet." But he answered them, "He who made me well was the one who said to me, 'Take up your pallet and walk.'" But he who was healed did not know who it was, for Jesus had slipped away while there was a crowd in that place. Afterward, Jesus found Him in the temple, and said to him, "Behold, you have become well, do not sin anymore so that nothing worse may befall you." The man ran away and told the Jews that it was Jesus who had made Him well. And the reason the Jews were persecuting Jesus because He was doing these things on the Sabbath. But He answered them, "My Father is working until now, and I Myself am working." For this cause, therefore the Jews were seeking all the more to kill Him because not only was He breaking the Sabbath, also calling God His own Father, making Himself equal with God.

Now it happened that while the crowd was pressing around Him, He saw two boats lying at the edge of the lake but the fishermen were not in them, they were washing their nets. And He got into Simon's boat and said, "Put out into deeper water and you will make a fine catch of fish." Simon replied, "Master worked hard all night and caught nothing, but as You say, we'll let the nets down." And after doing this the nets enclosed such a great quantity of fish that they began to tear. So they signaled to their partners in the other boat for them to come and help them. And they came and filled both of the boats, so that they began to sink. But when Simon Peter saw that, he fell down at Jesus' feet, saying, "Go away from me Lord, for I am a sinful man!" For amazement had seized him and all his companions because of the catch of fish which they had taken; and so also were James and John, sons of Zebedee, who were partners with Simon. And Jesus said to Simon, "Do not fear, from now on you will be catching men." When they had brought their boats to land, they left everything and followed Him.

WHILE HE WAS IN ONE OF the cities, there was a man covered with leprosy; and when he saw Jesus, he fell on his face and implored Him, saying, "Lord, if You are willing, You can make me clean." And He stretched out His hand and touched him, saying, "I am willing; be cleansed." And immediately the leprosy left him. And He ordered him to tell no one, "But go and show yourself to the priest and make an offering for your cleansing, just as Moses commanded, as a testimony to them." But the news about Him was spreading even farther, and large crowds were gathering to hear Him and to be healed of their sicknesses. But Jesus Himself would often slip away to the wilderness and pray.

One day He was teaching; and there were some Pharisees and teachers of the law sitting there, who had come from every village of Galilee and Judea and from Jerusalem; and the power of the Lord was present for Him to perform healing. And some men were carrying on a bed a man who was paralyzed; and they were trying to bring him in and to set him down in front of Him. But not finding any way to bring him in because of the crowd, they went up on the roof and let him down through the tiles with his stretcher, into the middle of the crowd, in front of

Jesus. Seeing their faith, He said, "Friend, your sins are forgiven you." The scribes and the Pharisees began to reason, saying, "Who is this man who speaks blasphemies? Who can forgive sins, but God alone?" But Jesus, aware of their reasonings, answered and said to them, "Why are you reasoning in your hearts? Which is easier, to say, 'Your sins have been forgiven you,' or to say, 'Get up and walk?' But, so that you may know that the Son of Man has authority on earth to forgive sins." He said to the paralytic, "I say to you, get up, and pick up your stretcher and go home." Immediately he got up before them, and picked up what he had been lying on, and went home glorifying God. They were all struck with astonishment and began glorifying God; and they were filled with fear, saying, "We have seen remarkable things today."

After that He went out and noticed a tax collector named Levi sitting in the tax booth, and He said to him, "Follow Me." And he left everything behind, and got up and began to follow Him. And Levi gave a big reception for Him in his house; and there was a great crowd of tax collectors and other people who were reclining at the table with them. The Pharisees and their scribes began grumbling at His disciples, saying, "Why do you eat and drink with the tax collectors and sinners?" And Jesus answered and said to them, "It is not those who are well who need a physician, but those who are sick. I have not come to call the righteous but sinners to repentance." And they said to Him, "The disciples of John often fast and offer prayers, the disciples of the Pharisees also do the same, but Yours eat and drink." And Jesus said to them, "You cannot make the attendants of the bridegroom fast while the bridegroom is with them, can you? But the days will come; and when the bridegroom is taken away from them, then they will fast in those days." And He was also telling them a parable: "No one tears a piece of cloth from a new garment and puts it on an old garment; otherwise he will both tear the new, and the piece from the new will not match the old. And no one puts new wine into old wineskins; otherwise the new wine will burst the skins and it will be spilled out, and the skins will be ruined. But new wine must be put into fresh wineskins. And no one, after drinking old wine wishes for new; for he says, 'The old is good enough.'"

Twelve

On the Sabbath they went into Capernaum and He entered the synagogue and began to teach. And they were amazed at His teaching because He taught as One with authority and not as the scribes. Just then there was a man with an unclean spirit and he cried out, saying, "What business do we have with each other, Jesus of Nazareth? Have You come to destroy us? I know who You are You are the Holy One of God!" And Jesus rebuked Him, saying "Be quiet and come out of Him!" Throwing Him into convulsions, the unclean spirit cried out with a loud voice and came out of Him. And they were all amazed, so the debated among themselves, saying, "What I this? A new teaching with authority? He commands even the unclean spirits and they obey Him!" Immediately the news about Him spread everywhere into all the surrounding districts of Galilee.

After returning from Capernaum, Jesus was at home and there were so many gathered there that there was no more room. And four men came, carrying a paralytic. And because there was no room they went up on the roof, dug an opening and lowered the man on a pallet. And Jesus, seeing their faith, said, "Son, your sins are forgiven." But some Scribes witnessed this and said to themselves, "How can this man do such a thing? It is blasphemy, only God can forgive sins." And he said to Him, "Teacher, I have kept all these things from my youth up." And looking at him, Jesus felt a love for him, "One thing you lack, go and sell all you possess and give to the poor, and you shall have treasure in heaven, and come, follow Me." But at these words, his face fell, and he went away grieved, for he was one who owned much property. And Jesus, looking around, said to His disciples, "How hard it will be for those who are wealthy to enter the kingdom of God. It is easier for a camel to go through the eye of a needle than for a rich man to enter the kingdom of God." And they were even more astonished and said to Him, "then who can be saved?" Looking at them, Jesus said, "With men it is impossible, but not with God, for all things are possible with God."

The disciples were amazed because in Judaism riches were a mark of God's favor and thus an advantage, not a barrier, in relation to God's kingdom. About the "needle," this is a familiar saying, an old Jewish proverb, spoken in humor, to describe something impossible. The camel was the largest animal in Palestine, and the word "needle" means a sewing needle, nothing more.

Peter began to say to Him, "Behold, we have left everything and followed You." Jesus said, "Truly I say to you there is no one who has left house or brothers or sisters or mother or father or children or farms, for My sake and for the sake of the gospel. But he shall receive a hundred times as much now in the present age, houses and brothers and sisters and mothers and children and farms, along with persecutions, and in the age to come, eternal life. But many who are first will be last, and the last, first."

So, here we have Peter popping off again, presumptuously reminding Jesus that we, unlike the rich man, have left every thing behind. And when Jesus says "no one," He is speaking of the twelve, knowing that they have given up their families and livelihoods for the sake of Jesus and His gospel. But to everyone who makes this break, Jesus promised that these things will be replaced a hundredfold by new ties with fellow disciples. The "age to come" of course is eternity and with it eternal life.

Jesus, aware of their thoughts said, "Why are you reasoning about things in your hearts? Which is easier to say to the paralytic, 'Your sins are forgiven,' or to say, 'Get up and walk?' But so that you may know that the Son of Man has authority on earth to forgive sins, I said to the man, 'Pick up your pallet and go home.'"

And the man did just that and walked out of sight of everyone so that they were all amazed and were glorifying God, saying, "We have never seen anything like this!"

WHEN JESUS ENTERED CAPERNAUM A CENTURION came to Him, imploring Him. "Lord, my servant is lying paralyzed at home, fearfully tormented." Jesus said, "I will come and heal Him." The centurion answered, "Lord, I am not worthy for You to come under my roof but just say the word and my servant will be healed. For I am also a man under authority, with soldiers under me, and I say to this one Go and he goes. Or I say 'Do this,' and he does it."

Now when Jesus heard this He marveled and He said to those who were following, "Truly I say to you I have not found such great faith with anyone in Israel." And He said to Him, "Go and it shall be done for you as you have believed." And the servant was healed that very moment.

AND THEY SAILED TO THE COUNTRY of the Gerasenes, which is opposite Galilee. And when they had come out onto the land, He was met by a certain man from the city who was possessed with demons, and who had not put on any clothing for a long time, and was not living in a house, but in the tombs. And seeing Jesus, he cried out and fell before Him and said in a loud voice, "What do I have to do with You, Jesus, Son of the Most High God? I beg You, do not torment me." For He had been commanding the unclean spirit to come out of the man. For it had seized him many times and he was bound with chains and shackles and kept under guard, and yet he would burst his fetters and be driven by the demon into the desert. And Jesus asked Him, "What is your name?" And he said, "Legion," for many demons had entered Him. And they were entreating Him not to command them to depart in to the abyss.

Even if the demoniac doesn't recognize Jesus, the demon does because the man cries out to him by name. Like all demoniacs he is unable to control himself and he shouted most of the time. When the man pleads that Jesus not torment him, this is the demon recognizing that Jesus could deal with him, even if the man could not by himself.

Now there was a herd of many swine feeding there on the mountain, and the demons entreated Him to permit them to enter the swine. And He gave them permission. And the demons came out of the man and entered the swine, and the herd rushed down the steep bank into the lake, and were drowned. And when the herdsmen saw what had happened, they ran away and reported it in the city and out in the country. And the people went out to see what had happened and they came to Jesus, and found the man from whom the demons had gone out, sitting down at the feet of Jesus, clothed and in his right mind, and they became frightened. And those who had seen it reported to them how the man who was demon-possessed had been made well. And all the people of the country of the Gerasenes and the surrounding district asked Him to depart from them, for they were gripped with fear, and He got into a boat and returned. But the man from whom the demons had gone out was begging Him that he might accompany Him, but He sent away, saying, "Return to your house and describe what great things God has done for you." And he went away, proclaiming throughout the whole city what great things Jesus had done for Him.

Soon afterwards He went to a city called Nain, and His disciples were going along with Him, accompanied by a large crowd. Now as He approached the gate of the city, a dead man was being carried out, the only son of his mother, and she was a widow, and a sizeable crowd from the city was with her. When the Lord saw her, He felt compassion for her, and said to her, "Do not weep." And He came and touched the coffin, and the bearers came to a halt. And He said, "Young man, I say to you 'arise.'" The dead man began to speak, and Jesus gave him back to his mother. Great fear gripped them all, and they began glorifying God, saying, "A great prophet has arisen among us. God has visited His people!" This report concerning Him went out all over Judea and in the surrounding district.

Now when Jesus saw a crowd around Him, He gave orders to depart to the other side of the sea. When He got into the boat, His disciples followed Him. And, behold, there arose a great storm on the sea so that the boat was being covered with the waves, but Jesus Himself was asleep. And they came to Him and woke Him, saying, "Save us Lord, we are perishing!" He said to them, "Why are you afraid, you men of little faith?" Then He got up and rebuked the winds and the sea and it became perfectly calm. The men were amazed and said, "What kind of man is this, that even the winds and sea obey Him?"

And He summoned the twelve and began to send them out in pairs, and gave them authority over the unclean spirits. And He instructed them that they should take nothing except a staff—no bread and no money, "but do wear sandals and only one tunic. And whenever you enter a house, stay there. And any place that does not receive you, shake the dust off your feet as a testimony against them."

They went out and preached that men should repent. They cast out demons and anointed with oil many sick people and healed them.

Thirteen

And King Herod had heard of Jesus, for His name had become well known. And people were saying, "John the Baptist has risen from the dead and that is why these miraculous powers are at work in Him." Others were saying, "He is Elijah," others said "He is a prophet, like one of our prophets of old." But when Herod heard of it, he kept saying, "John, whom I beheaded, has risen!"

Jesus went away to the other side of the sea and a large crowd followed Him. Then He went up on a hillside and His disciples followed Him. He said to Phillip, "Where are to buy bread that these may eat?" Phillip answered, "Two hundred denarii worth of bread is not enough." Another of the disciples said, "There is a lad over here who has five barely loaves and two fish." Jesus said, "Have the people sit down." So the men sat, about 5,000 of them. Then Jesus took the loaves, gave thanks, and distributed to those who were seated, the fish, too, as much as they wanted. When they were filled, He said to His disciples, "Gather up the leftover fragments so that nothing will be lost." So, they gathered them up and filled twelve baskets with fragments left over from the barely loaves which had not been eaten. Therefore, when the people saw the miracle which He had performed, they said, Truly this is the Prophet who has come into the world. So Jesus, perceiving that they intended to take Him by force to make Him king, withdrew again to a certain place by Himself, alone.

NOW THERE WAS A MAN NAMED Jarius, an official of the synagogue. He sought out Jesus and told Him that his 12-year-old daughter was dying. Then someone came from his house and said, "Your daughter has died; don't trouble the Teacher any more." But when Jesus heard this, He said, "Don't be afraid, only believe that she will be made well." Now when He came to the house, He entered the child's room and found them weeping and lamenting for her. Then He said, "Stop weeping for she has not died but is asleep." And they laughed at Him knowing she had died. And He took her hand and said, "Child, arise!" And she awakened. Her parents were amazed but told them not to say anything about what had happened. These things He said in the synagogue as He taught in Capernaum. "But there are some of you who do not believe. For this reason I have said to you that no one can come to Me unless it has been granted Him from the Father." Because of this many disciples withdrew and did not follow Him any more. So Jesus said to the twelve, "You do not want to go away also, do you?" Simon Peter answered Him, "Lord, to whom shall we go? You have the words of eternal life. We have believed and come to know that You are the Holy one of God."

When John says that "many disciples withdrew and did not follow Him any more," we can't know how many people decided to give up on Jesus. There might have been only a few or hundreds. There were two reasons for their leaving: One, they had come to realize that Jesus' mission on earth was NOT to free Israel from the Roman yoke; there was absolutely nothing in His ministry of a political nature. The other reason had to do with what Jesus had said moments earlier, also recorded in John's gospel and we are familiar with these words: "Truly I say to you that unless you eat the flesh of the Son of Man and drink His blood, you have no life in yourselves. He who eats my flesh and drinks my blood will have eternal life and I will raise Him up on the last day."

Very difficult words indeed and if those who left Jesus had not been with Him for some time, it's easy to see why these words put them off.

He answered and said, "And who is He, Lord, that I may believe in Him?" Jesus said to Him, "You have both seen Him and He is the one who is talking with you." And he said, "Lord, I believe," and he worshiped Him. And Jesus said, "For judgment I came into the world, that those who do not see may see, and that those who see may become blind." Those of the Pharisees who were with Him heard these things and said to Him, "We are not blind too, are we?" Jesus said to them, "If you were blind you would have no sin, but since you say, 'We see,' your sin remains."

AND IT CAME ABOUT WHILE HE was on His way to Jerusalem, that He was passing between Samaria and Galilee. And as He entered a certain village ten leprous men who stood at a distance met Him and they raised their voices, saying, "Jesus, Master, have mercy on us." And when He saw them He said to them, "Go and show yourselves to the priests." And it came about that as they were going they were cleansed. Now one of them, when he saw that he had been healed, turned back, glorifying God with a loud voice, and he fell on his face at His feet giving thanks to Him. And he was a Samaritan.

And Jesus answered and said, "Were there not ten cleansed? But the nine, where are they? Was no one found who turned back to give glory to God, except this foreigner?" And He said to them, "Rise, and go your way. Your faith has made you well."

And behold, a certain lawyer stood up and put Him to the test, saying, "Teacher, what shall I do to inherit eternal life?" And He said to him, "What is written in the Law? How does it read to you?" And he answered and said, "You shall love the Lord your God with all your heart, and with all your soul and with all your mind, and your neighbor as yourself." And He said to him, "You have answered correctly, do this and you will live."

And wishing to justify himself, he said to Jesus, "And who is my neighbor?" Jesus replied and said, "A certain man was going down from Jerusalem to Jericho and fell among robbers who stripped him and beat him and went off leaving Him for dead. And by chance a certain priest was going down on that road and when he saw him he passed boy on the other side. And likewise a Levite also, when he came to the place and saw him, passed by on the other side. Then a certain Samaritan, who was on a journey, came upon him and when he saw him he felt compassion and came to him and bandage up his wounds, pouring oil and wine on them, and he put him on his own beast, brought him to an inn and took care of him. And on the next day he took out two denarii and gave them to the inn keeper and said, 'Take care of him and whatever you spend when I return, I will repay you.' Which of these three do you think proved to be a neighbor to the man who fell into the robbers' hands?" And he said, "The one who showed mercy to him." And Jess said to him, "Go and do the same."

Some local knowledge is helpful here. The road from Jerusalem to Jericho descends about 3,000 feet in 17 miles, steep and dangerous and robbers took advantage of this. And everyone hearing this conversation knew that. Also, we should know by now that the Samaritans were not well liked. The were scorned by the Jews because of their mixed Jewish and Gentile ancestry. And we should see some irony here, in that this Samaritan would help a half-dead Jew, not only on the spot but also in the future, as he told the innkeeper he would back to cover any further costs.

Fourteen

Now all the tax gatherers and sinners were coming near Him to listen to Him. And both the Pharisees and scribes began to grumble, saying, "This man receives sinners and eats with them." And He told them this parable, saying: "Which man among you, if he has a hundred sheep and has lost one of them, does not leave the ninety-nine in the open pasture and go after the one which is lost, until he finds it? And when he has found it, he lays it on his shoulders, rejoicing. And when he comes home he calls together his friends and his neighbors saying, 'Rejoice with me for I have found my sheep which was lost!' I tell you that in this same way there will be more joy in heaven over one sinner who repents, than over ninety-nine righteous persons who need no repentance. Or what woman, if she has ten silver coins and loses one coin, does not light a lamp and sweep the house and search carefully until she finds it? And when she has found it, she calls together her friends, saying, 'Rejoice with me for I have found the coin which I had lost!' In the same way, I tell you there is joy in the presence of the angles of God over one sinner who repents."

To further illustrate the point, He told them this story: "A man had two sons. When the younger told his father, 'I want my share of your estate now, instead of waiting until you die!' his father agreed to divide his wealth between his sons. A few days later this younger son packed all his belongings and took a trip to a distant land, and there wasted all his money on parties and prostitutes. About the time his money was gone a great famine swept over the land, and he began to starve. He persuaded a local farmer to hire him to feed his pigs. The boy became so hungry that even the pods he was feeding the swine looked good to him. And no one gave him anything. When he finally came to his senses, he said to Himself, 'At home even the hired men have food enough and to spare, and here I am, dying of hunger! I will go home to my father and say, 'Father, I have sinned against both heaven and you, and am no longer worthy of being called your son. Please take me on as a hired man.' So he returned home to his father. And while he was still a long distance away, his father saw him coming, and was filled with loving pity and ran and embraced him and kissed him. His son said to him, 'Father, I have sinned against heaven and you, and am not worthy of being called your son.' But his father said to the slaves, 'Quick! Bring the finest robe in the house and put it on him. And a jeweled ring for his finger; and shoes! And kill the calf we have in the fattening pen. We must celebrate with a feast, for this son of mine was dead and has returned to life. He was lost and is found.' So the party began. Meanwhile, the older son was in the fields working; when he returned home, he heard dance music coming from the house, and he asked one of the servants what was going on. 'Your brother is back,' he was told, 'and your father has killed the calf we were fattening and has prepared a great feast to celebrate his coming home again unharmed.' The older brother was angry and wouldn't go in. His father came out and begged him, but he replied, 'All these years I've worked hard for you and never once refused to do a single thing you told me to; and in all that time you never gave me even one young goat for a feast with my friends. Yet when this son of yours comes back after spending your money on prostitutes, you celebrate by killing the finest calf we have on the place.' 'Look, dear son,' his father said to him, 'you and I are very close, and everything I have is yours. But it is right to celebrate. For he is your brother; and he was dead and has come back to life! He was lost and is found!'

"And someone in the crowd said to Him, 'Teacher, tell my brother to divide the family inheritance with me.' But He said to him, 'Man who appointed Me to be a judge or arbiter over you?' And He said to them, 'Beware, and be on your guard against every form of greed, for not even when one has an abundance does his life consist of possessions.' And He told them a parable saying, 'The land of a rich man was very productive.' And he began reasoning to himself saying, 'What shall I do for I have no place to store my crops?' And he said, 'This is what I will do. I will tear down by barns and build larger ones, and there I will store all my grain and goods. And I will say to my soul, 'Soul, you have much goods laid up for many years; take your ease, eat, drink, be merry.' But God said unto him, 'you foolish one, this night is your soul required of you; and the things which you have prepared, whose shall they be? So is he that lays up treasure for himself, and is not rich toward God.' And He said unto His disciples, Therefore I say unto you, 'Be not anxious for your life, what you shall eat; nor clothes for your body, what you shall put on. For the life is more than the food, and the body than the raiment. Consider the ravens, that they sow not, neither reap; which have no store-chamber nor barn; and God feeds them: of how much more value are you than the birds! And which of you by being anxious can add a cubit unto the measure of his life? If then you are not able to do even that which is least, why are you anxious concerning the rest? Consider the lilies, how they grow: they toil not, neither do they spin; yet I say unto you, Even Solomon in all his glory was not arrayed like one of these. But if God so clothes the grass in the field, which to-day is, and tomorrow is cast into the oven; how much more shall he clothe you, O you of little faith? And seek not you what you shall eat, and what you shall drink, neither be you of doubtful mind. For all these things do the nations of the world seek after: but your Father knows that you have need of these things. You seek you his kingdom, and these things shall be added unto you. Fear not, little flock; for it is your Father's good pleasure to give you the kingdom. Sell that which you have, and give alms; make for yourselves purses which wax not old, a treasure in the heavens that does not fail, where no thief draws near, neither moth destroys. For where your treasure is, there will your heart be also. Let your loins be girded about, and your lamps burning; and be you yourselves like unto men looking for their lord, when he shall return from the marriage feast; that, when he comes and knocks, they may straightway open unto Him. Blessed are those servants, whom the lord when he comes shall find watching: verily I say unto you, that he shall gird himself, and make them sit down to eat, and shall come and serve them. And if he shall come in the second watch, and if in the third, and find them so blessed are those *servants*. But know this, that if the master of the house had known in what hour the thief was coming, he would have watched, and not have left his house to be broken through. Be you also ready: for in an hour that you think not the Son of man has come.'"

And Peter said, "Lord, do you speak this parable unto us, or even unto all?" And the Lord said, "Who then is the faithful and wise steward, whom his lord shall set over his household, to give them their portion of food in due season? Blessed is that servant, whom his lord when he comes shall find so doing. Of a truth I say unto you, that he will set him over all that he has. But if that servant shall say in his heart, My lord delays his coming; and shall begin to beat the menservants and the maidservants, and to eat and drink, and to be drunken; the lord of that servant shall come in a day when he expects not, and in an hour when he knows not, and shall cut him asunder, and appoint his portion with the unfaithful. And that servant, who knew his lord's will, and made not ready, nor did according to his will, shall be beaten with many stripes; but he that knew not, and did things worthy of stripes, shall be beaten with few stripes. And to whomsoever much is given, of him shall much be required: and to whom they commit much, of him will they ask the more. I came to cast fire upon the earth; and what do I desire, if it is already kindled? But I have a baptism to be baptized with; and how am I straitened till it be accomplished! Think you that I am come to give peace in the earth? I tell you, Nay; but rather division: or there shall be from henceforth five in one house divided, three against two, and two against three. They shall be divided, father against son, and son against father; mother against daughter, and daughter against her mother; mother-in-law against her daughter-in-law, and daughter-in-law against her mother-in-law." And He said to the multitudes also, "When you see a cloud rising in the west, immediately you say, 'There comes a shower,' and so it comes to pass. And when you see a south wind blowing, you say, 'There will be a scorching heat,' and it comes to pass. You hypocrites, you know how to interpret the face of the earth and the heaven; but how is it that you know not how to interpret this time? And who among yourselves judge you not what is right? Or as you are going with your adversary before the magistrate, on the way give diligence to be rid of him, lest haply he drag you unto the judge, and the judge shall deliver you to the officer, and the officer shall put you in prison. I say unto you, 'you shall by no means come out then, till you have paid the very last mite.'"

Fifteen

He entered Jericho and was passing through. And there was a man by the name of Zaccheus, he was a chief tax collector and he was rich. Zaccheus was trying to see who Jesus was, and was unable because of the crowd, for he was small in stature. So he ran on ahead and climbed into a sycamore tree in order to see Him, for He was about to pass through that way. When Jesus came to the place, He looked up and said Him, "Zaccheus, hurry and come down, for today I must stay at your house." And he hurried and came down and received Him gladly. When they saw Him they began to grumble, saying, "He has gone to be the guest of a man who is a sinner." Zaccheus stopped and said to the Lord, "Behold, half of my possessions I will give tot the poor, and if I have defrauded anyone of anything, I will give back four times as much." And Jesus said to him, "Today salvation has come to this house, because he, too, is a son of Abraham. For the Son of Man has come to save that which was lost."

Now a certain man was sick, Lazarus of Bethany, the village of Mary and her sister Martha. And it was Mary who anointed the Lord with ointment, and wiped His feet with her hair, whose brother Lazarus was sick.

There is something about these two verses that readers should understand. The apostle John wants his readers to know WHICH Mary he's writing about, knowing there are several other women of the same name in Jesus' life. Also, in those days people didn't have first and last names. Often, the person was identified by his/her name and the town or village where he/she lived.

The sisters therefore sent to Him, saying, "Lord, behold, he whom You love is sick." But when Jesus heard it He said, "This sickness is not unto death, but for the glory of God, that the Son of God may be glorified by it." Now Jesus loved Martha, and her sister and Lazarus. When He had heard that he was sick, He stayed there two days longer in the place where He was. Then after this He said to the disciples, "Let us go to Judea again." The disciples said to Him, "Rabbi, the Jews just now were seeking to stone You and You are going there again?" Jesus answered, "Are there not twelve hours in the day? If anyone walks in the day, he does not stumble because he sees the light of the world. But if anyone walks in the night, he stumbles, because the light is not in Him."

Why do we suppose that Jesus stayed two more days rather than hurrying to Bethany? Lazarus probably was dead when Jesus received the message, but He was working according to God's plan. He wanted Lazarus to have been "dead" for a few days so that everyone would see the impact of what He planned to do. Also, what is the point of Jesus' hyperbole about twelve hours in a day? Jesus spoke in a veiled way to illustrate that it would NOT be too dangerous to go to Bethany. In one sense He was speaking of walking—or living—in physical light or darkness. In the spiritual realm, when one lives by the will of God, that is "in the light," he is safe. But living in the realm of evil—in the night—as Jesus puts it, is not safe.

This He said, and after that He told them, "Our friend Lazarus has fallen asleep, but I go that I may awaken Him out of sleep." The disciples said to Him, "Lord, if he has fallen asleep, he will recover." Now Jesus had spoken of his death, but they thought that He was speaking of literal sleep. Then Jesus said to them, "Lazarus is dead, and I am glad for you sakes that I was not there, so that you may believe, but let us go to Him." Thomas, therefor, who is called Didymus, said to his fellow disciples, "Let us also go, that we may be with Him." So when Jesus came he found that he already been in the tomb four days. Now Bethany was near Jerusalem, about two miles off and many of the Jews had come to Martha and Mary to console them regarding their brother. Martha, therefore, when she heard that Jesus was coming went to meet Him, but Mary still sat in the house.

Martha said to Jesus, "Lord, if you had been here my brother would not have died. Even now I know that whatever You ask of God, God will give You." Jesus said to her, "Your brother will rise again." Martha said to Him, "I know that he will rise again in the resurrection of the last day." Jesus said to her, "I am the resurrection and the life; He who believes in Me shall live even if he dies. And everyone who lives and believes in Me shall never die. Do you believe this?"

She said to Him, "Yes, Lord, I have believed that You are the Christ, the Son of God, even He who comes into the world." And when she had said this, she went away, and called Mary, her sister, saying secretly, "The Teacher is here and is calling for you." And when she heard it, she arose quicky and was coming to Him. Now Jesus had not yet come into the village, but was still in the place were Martha met Him. The Jews then who were with her in the house, and consoling her, when they saw that Mary rose up quickly and went out, followed her, supposing she was going to the tomb to weep there. Therefore, when Mary came where Jesus was, she saw Him and fell at His feet, saying, "Lord, if you had been here, my brother would not have died." When Jesus saw her weeping, and the Jews who came with her also weeping, He was deeply moved in spirit, and was troubled, and said, "Where have you laid Him?" They said, to Him, "Lord come and see." Jesus wept.

There is more to this text that meets the eye, unless we have access to the original Greek and can read it. Mary is showing her faith, although it is a limited faith, as her sister had shown moments earlier. But the English words "deeply moved," and "troubled," don't convey the whole picture. "Deeply moved" really means "angered" and "troubled" means "agitated" as a pool of water. It seems likely that Jesus felt these emotions because He was angry at the tyranny of Satan who had brought death and sorrow to people, and agitated because of His ongoing conflict with sin, death and Satan. And lest we forget, we all know that verse 35 is the shortest verse in the English Bible. What we may not know is that in the original Greek, the verb means a "quiet shedding of tears," in contrast to the loud wailings of the crowd. They interpreted His tears as an expression of love, or frustration at not being able to heal Lazarus.

And so the Jews were saying, "Behold, how He loved Him!" But some of them said, "Could not this man, who opened the eyes of Him who was blind, have kept this man from dying?" Jesus again being deeply moved within, came to the tomb. Now it was in a cave, and a stone was lying against it. Jesus said, "Remove the stone." Martha, the sister of the deceased, said to Him, "Lord, by this time there will be a stench for he has been dead for four days." Jesus said to her, "Did I not say to you, if you believe, you will see the glory of God?" And so they removed the stone and Jesus raised His eyes and said, "Father, I thank Thee that Thou heard me. And I know that Thou hears Me always, but because of the people standing here, I said that they may believe that Thou did send Me." And when He had said these things, He cried out in a loud voice, "Lazarus, come forth!" He who had died came forth, bound hand and foot with wrappings, and his face was wrapped around with a cloth. Jesus said to them, "Unbind Him and let him go."

Many of the Jews, who had come to Mary and beheld what He had done, believed in Him. But some of them went away to the Pharisees and told them the things which Jesus had done. So the chief priests and the Pharisees convened a council and were saying, "What are we doing? For this man is performing many signs. If we let Him go on like this, all men will believe in Him, and the Romans will come and take away both our place and our nation." But a certain one of them, Caiaphas, who was high priest that year, said to them, "You know nothing at all, nor do you take into account that it is expedient for you that one man should die for the people, and that the whole nation should not perish." Now this he said on his own initiative, but being high priest that year, he prophesied that Jesus was going to die for the nation, and not only for the nation, but that he might also gather together into one the children of God who are scattered abroad. So from that day on they planned together to kill Him.

A word about Caiaphas: years earlier, the High Priest was appointed for life, but later the Romans decided that the arrangement placed too much power into the hands of one man, so they began limiting the term of office. Caiaphas, extra-biblical records tell us, served in this capacity from AD 18 to 36, which is another way we can fix the time of Jesus' public ministry.

Sixteen

And as He passed by, He saw a man blind from birth. And His disciples asked Him, "Rabbi, who sinned, this man or his parents, that he must be born blind?" Jesus answered, "It was neither that this man sinned, nor his parents, but in order that the works of God might be displayed in Him. We must work the works of Him who sent Me, as long as it is day, night is coming, when no man can work. While I am in the world, I am the light of the world." When He had said this, He spat on the ground, and made clay of the spittle, and applied the clay to his eyes, and said, "Go wash in the pool of Siloam." And so he went away and washed, and came back seeing. The neighbors, therefore, and those who previously saw him as a beggar, were saying, "Is this not the one who used to sit and beg?" Others were saying, "This is he," still others were saying, "No, but he is like Him." He kept saying, "I am the one." Therefore they were saying to Him, "How then were your eyes opened?" He answered, "The man who is called Jesus made clay and anointed my eyes, and said to me, 'Go to Siloam and wash,' so I went there and washed and received my sight." And they said to Him, "Where is He?" He said, "I do not know." They brought to the Pharisees him was formerly blind.

Now it was the Sabbath on the day when Jesus made the clay and opened his eyes. Again, the Pharisees also were asking Him how e received his sight, and he said to them, "He applied clay to my eyes and I washed and I see." So some of the Pharisees were saying, "This man is not from God because He does not keep the Sabbath." But others were saying, "How can a man who is a sinner perform such signs?" And there was a division among them. They said to the blind man again, "What do you say about Him since He opened your eyes?" And he said, "He is a prophet." The Jews did not believe it of Him, that he had been blind and had received sight, until they called the parents of the one who had received his sight, and questioned them, saying "Is this your son, who you say was born blind? Then how does he now see?" The parents answered them and said, "We know that this is our son, and that he was born blind. Then how does he now see?" His parents answered them and said, "We know that he is our son and that he was born blind, but how he now sees we do not know who opened his eyes. Ask him, he is of age, he will speak for himself." His parents said this because they were afraid of the Jews.

They said to Him, "What did He do to you? How did He open your eyes?" He answered them, "I told you already, and you did not listen. Why do you want to hear it again? You do not want to become His disciples, do you?" And they reviled him and said, "You are His disciple, but we are disciples of Moses. We know that God has spoken to Moses, but as for this man, we do not know where He is from." The man answered and said, "Well, here is an amazing thing, that you do not know where He is from, and yet He opened my eyes. We know that God does not hear sinners; but if anyone is God-fearing and does His will, He hears Him. Since the beginning of time it has never been heard that anyone opened the eyes of a person born blind. If this man were not from God, He could do nothing." They answered him, "You were born entirely in sins, and are you teaching us?" So they put him out. Jesus heard that they had put him out, and finding him, He said, "Do you believe in the Son of Man?" He answered, "Who is He, Lord, that I may believe in Him?" Jesus said to Him, "You have both seen Him, and He is the one who is talking with you." And he said, "Lord, I believe." And he worshiped Him. And Jesus said, "For judgment I came into this world, so that those who do not see may see, and that those who see may become blind." Those of the Pharisees who were with Him heard these things and said to Him, "We are not blind too, are we?" Jesus said to them, "If you were blind, you would have no sin; but since you say, 'We see,' your sin remains." And many believed in Him.

The neighbors, and those who previously saw him as beggar, were saying, "Is this not the one who used to sit and beg?" Others were saying, "This is he," still others were saying, "No, but he is like him." He kept saying, "I am the one." Therefore, they were saying to him, "How then were your eyes opened?" He answered, "The man who is called Jesus made clay and anointed my eyes and said 'Go wash in the pool of Siloam,' so I went away and washed and received my sight." And they said to Him, "Where is He?" He said, "I do not know."

They brought him to the Pharisees, he who was formerly blind. Now it was the Sabbath on the day that Jesus made the clay and opened his eyes. Again, the Pharisees were asking Him how he received his sight, and he said to them, "He applied clay to my eyes and I washed, and I see." So, some of the Pharisees were saying, "This man is not from God because He does not keep the Sabbath." But others were saying, "How can a man who is a sinner perform such signs?" And there was a division among them.

They said to the blind man again, "What do you say about Him, since He opened your eyes?" And he said, "He is a prophet." The Jews did not believe him, that he had been blind and recovered his sight, until they called the parents of the one who had received his sight, and questioned them, saying, "Is this your son, who you say was born blind? Then how does he now see?" His parents answered them and said, "We know that this is our son and that he was born blind, but how he now sees, we do not know, or who opened his eyes, we do not know. Ask him, he is of age and can speak for himself." His parents said this because they were afraid of the Jews; for the Jews had already agreed that if anyone confessed Him to be Christ, he was to be put out of the synagogue. For this reason his parents said, "He is of age; ask Him." So a second time they called the man who had been blind, and said to Him, "Give glory to God; we know that this man is a sinner." He then answered, "Whether He is a sinner, I do not know; one thing I do know, that though I was blind, now I see." So they said to Him, "What did He do to you? How did He open your eyes?" He answered them, "I told you already and you did not listen; why do you want to hear it again? You do not want to become His disciples too, do you?" They reviled Him and said, "You are His disciple, but we are disciples of Moses. We know that God has spoken to Moses, but as for this man, we do not know where He is from." The man answered and said to them, "Well, here is an amazing thing, that you do not know where He is from, and He opened my eyes. We know that God does not hear sinners; but if anyone is God-fearing and does His will, He hears him. Since the beginning of time it has never been heard that anyone opened the eyes of a person born blind. If this man were not from God, He could do nothing." They answered Him, "You were born entirely in sins, and are you teaching us?" So they put Him out.

Jesus heard that they had put him out, and finding him, He said, "Do you believe in the Son of Man?" He answered, "Who is He, Lord, that I may believe in Him?" Jesus said to Him, "You have both seen Him, and He is the one who is talking with you."

And he said, "Lord, I believe." And he worshiped Him. And Jesus said, "For judgment I came into this world, so that those who do not see may see, and that those who see may become blind." Those of the Pharisees who were with Him heard these things and said to Him, "We are not blind too, are we?" Jesus said to them, "If you were blind, you would have no sin; but since you say, 'We see,' your sin remains."

Seventeen

And when they had approached Jerusalem and had come to Bethpage, to the Mount of Olives, then Jesus sent two disciples saying to them, "Go into the village and you will find a donkey tied there and a colt with her, untie them and bring them to Me. If anyone says something to you, you shall say 'the Lord has need of them,' and immediately he will send them."

Now this took place that what was through the prophet might be fulfilled, saying: "Say to the daughter of Zion, 'behold, your King is coming to you, gentle and mounted on a donkey, even on a colt, the foal of a beast of burden.'" And the disciples went and did just as Jesus had directed them and brought the donkey and the colt, and laid on them their garments, on which He sat. Most of the crowd spread their coats on the road and others were cutting branches of trees. The crowds going ahead of Him, and those who followed, shouted, "Hosanna, to the Son of David, blessed is he who comes in the name of the Lord."

When He entered Jerusalem, all the city was stirred, asking "Who is this?" And the crowds were saying, "This is the Prophet Jesus, from Nazareth in Galilee."

And they came to Jerualem and He entered the temple and began to cast out those who were buying and selling in the temple, and overturned the tables of the money changers and the seats of those who were selling doves. And He would not permit anyone to carry goods through the temple. And He began to teach and say to them, "Is it not written, 'My house shall be called a house of prayer for all the nations?' But you have made it a robber's den."

And the chief priests and scribes began seeking how to destroy Him. For they were afraid of Him, for all the multitude was astounded at His teaching.

"He who has the bride is the bridegroom, but the friend of the bridegroom, who stands and hears him, he rejoices greatly because of the bridegroom's voice. And so this joy of mine has been made full. He must increase, but I must decrease. He who comes from above is above all."

And He also said to disciples, "There was a certain rich man, who had a steward; and the same was accused unto Him that he was wasting his goods. And he called him, and said to him, 'What is this that I hear of you? render the account of your stewardship; for you can no longer be a steward.'

"And the steward said within himself, 'What shall I do, seeing that my lord takes away the stewardship from me? I have not strength to dig; to beg I am ashamed. I am resolved what to do, that, when I am put out of the stewardship, they may receive me into their houses.' And calling to him each one of his lord's debtors, he said to the first, 'How much do you owe my lord?' And he said, 'A hundred measures of oil.' And he said unto Him, 'Take your bond, and sit down quickly and write fifty.' Then said he to another, 'And how much do you owe?' And he said, 'A hundred measures of wheat.' He said to him, 'Take your bond, and write fourscore.' And his lord commended the unrighteous steward because he had done wisely: for the sons of this world are for their own generation wiser than the sons of the light. And I say unto you, 'Make to yourselves friends by means of the mammon of unrighteousness; that, when it shall fail, they may receive you into the eternal tabernacles. He that is faithful in a very little is faithful also in much: and he that is unrighteous in a very little is unrighteous also in much.'

"If therefore you have not been faithful in the unrighteous mammon, who will commit to your trust the true riches? And if you have not been faithful in that which is another's, who will give you that which is your own?

"No servant can serve two masters: for either he will hate the one, and love the other; or else he will hold to one, and despise the other. You cannot serve God and mammon." And the Pharisees, who were lovers of money, heard all these things; and they scoffed at Him.

And He said to them, "You are they that justify yourselves in the sight of men; but God knows your hearts: for that which is exalted among men is an abomination in the sight of God. The law and the prophets were until John: from that time the gospel of the kingdom of God is preached, and every man enters violently into it. But it is easier for heaven and earth to pass away, than for one tittle of the law to fall. Every one that puts away his away his wife, and marries another, commits adultery: and he that marries one that is put away from a husband commits adultery."

WHAT FOLLOWS IS THE CONCLUSION OF *Luke's gospel. It is much different from Matthew's account but nonetheless compelling. It is the well-know* Road to Emmaus *story, admired by Christians everywhere.*

And behold, two of them were going that very day to a village named Emmaus, which was about seven miles from Jerusalem.

And they were talking with each other about all these things which had taken place. While they were talking and discussing, Jesus Himself approached and began traveling with them. But their eyes were prevented from recognizing Him. And He said to them, "What are these words that you are exchanging with one another as you are walking?" And they stood still, looking sad. One of them, named Cleopas, answered and said to Him, "Are You the only one visiting Jerusalem and unaware of the things which have happened here in these days?" And He said to them, "What things?" And they said to Him, "The things about Jesus the Nazarene, who was a prophet mighty in deed and word in the sight of God and all the people, and how the chief priests and our rulers delivered Him to the sentence of death, and crucified Him. But we were hoping that it was He who was going to redeem Israel. Indeed, besides all this, it is the third day since these things happened. But also some women among us amazed us. When they were at the tomb early in the morning, and did not find His body, they came, saying that they had also seen a vision of angels who said that He was alive. Some of those who were with us went to the tomb and found it just exactly as the women also had said; but Him they did not see." And He said to them, "O foolish men and slow of heart to believe in all that the prophets have spoken! Was it not necessary for the Christ to suffer these things and to enter into His glory?"

Then beginning with Moses and with all the prophets, He explained to them the things concerning Himself in all the Scriptures. And they approached the village where they were going, and He acted as though He were going farther. But they urged Him, saying, "Stay with us, for it is getting toward evening, and the day is now nearly over." So He went in to stay with them. When He had reclined at the table with them, He took the bread and blessed it, and breaking it, He began giving it to them. Then their eyes were opened and they recognized Him; and He vanished from their sight. They said to one another, "Were not our hearts burning within us while He was speaking to us on the road, while He was explaining the Scriptures to us?" And they got up that very hour and returned to Jerusalem, and found gathered together the eleven and those who were with them, saying, "The Lord has really risen and has appeared to Simon."

They began to relate their experiences on the road and how He was recognized by them in the breaking of the bread. And as they spoke these things, He Himself stood in the midst of them, and said to them, 'Peace be unto you.' But they were terrified and frightened, and supposed that they beheld a spirit. And He said to them, 'Why are you troubled? and why do these questions arise in your heart? See my hands and my feet, that it is I myself: handle me, and see; for a spirit does not have flesh and bones, as you see Me having.'

And when He had said this, he showed them his hands and his feet. And while they still disbelieved for joy, and wondered, He said unto them, 'Have you here anything to eat?' And they gave him a piece of a broiled fish. And He took it, and ate before them. And He said unto them, 'These are my words which I spoke to you, while I was yet with you, that all things must be fulfilled, which are written in the law of Moses, and the prophets, and the psalms, concerning Me." Then He opened their minds, that they might understand the scriptures; and He said unto them, 'Thus it is written, that the Christ should suffer, and rise again from the dead the third day; and that repentance and remission of sins should be preached in his name unto all the nations, beginning from Jerusalem. You are witnesses of these things. And behold, I send forth the promise of my Father upon you: but wait in the city, until you be clothed with power from on high.'

And he led them out until they were near Bethany: and he lifted up his hands, and blessed them. And it came to pass, while He blessed them, He parted from them, and was carried up into heaven. And they worshipped him, and returned to Jerusalem with great joy: And they were continually in the temple, blessing God.

Eighteen

Let's pause for a moment so that readers may see what the fourth Gospel writer has to say. That would be the Apostle John.

When the Lord knew that the Pharisees had heard that Jesus was making and baptizing more disciples than John (although Jesus himself baptized not, but his disciples), he left Judea, and departed again into Galilee. And he had to pass through Samaria. So he came to a city of Samaria, called Sychar, near to the parcel of ground that Jacob gave to his son Joseph: and Jacob's well was there. Jesus was tired from his journey and sat by the well. It was about the sixth hour. There came a woman of Samaria to draw water: Jesus said to her, to her, Give me a drink. For his disciples had gone into the city to buy food. The Samaritan woman said to him, How is it that you, being a Jew, asks me, who am a Samaritan woman? (For Jews have no dealings with Samaritans.) Jesus answered and said unto to her, "If you know the gift of God, and who it is that says to you, 'Give me to drink,' you would have asked of him, and he would have given you living water." The woman said to him, "Sir, you have nothing to draw with, and the well is deep: from where to you have that living water? Are you greater than our father Jacob, who gave us the well, and drank from it himself, and his sons and his cattle?" Jesus answered and said to her, "Every one that drinks this water shall thirst again: but whoever drinks of the water that I shall give him shall never thirst; but the water that I shall give him shall become in him a well of water springing up unto eternal life." The woman said to him, "Sir, give me this water, that I will not thirst, neither come all the way here to draw." Jesus said to her, "Go, call your husband, and come here." The woman answered and said to him, "I have no husband." Jesus said to her, "you say it well, that, I have no husband: for you have had five husbands; and he whom you now have is not your husband; this you have said correctly." The woman said to him, "Sir, I believe that you are a prophet. Our fathers worshipped on this mountain; and you say, that in Jerusalem is the place where men ought to worship." Jesus said to her, "Woman, believe me, the hour has come when neither on this mountain, nor in Jerusalem, shall you worship the Father. You worship that which you don't know, but we worship that which we know; for salvation is from the Jews. But the hour comes, and now is, when the true worshippers shall worship the Father in spirit and truth: for such does the Father seek to be his worshippers. God is a Spirit: and they that worship him must worship in spirit and truth." The woman said to him, "I know that Messiah comes (he that is called Christ): when he has come, he will declare unto us all things." Jesus said to her, "I that speak to you am he." And then came his disciples; and they marveled that he was speaking with a woman; yet no man said, "What are you looking for? Why do you speak with her?" So the woman left her waterpot, and went away into the city, and told the people, "Come, see a man, who told me all things that I ever did. Can this be the Christ?" They went out of the city, and were coming to him.

Meanwhile, the disciples prayed with him, saying, "Rabbi, eat." But he said to them, "I have a task that you know nothing about." Jesus said to them, "My task is to do the will of him who sent me, and to accomplish his work. Don't say there are yet four months, and then comes the harvest. He that reaps receives wages and gathers fruit unto life eternal; that he that sows and he that reaps may rejoice together. For hear the truth: One sows, and another reaps. I sent you to reap that whereon you have not labored: others have labored, and you are entered into their labor."

And from that city many of the Samaritans believed in him because of the word of the woman, who testified, "He told me all things that ever I did." So when the Samaritans came to him, they begged him to stay with them: and he stayed there two days. And many more believed because of his word; and they said to the woman, "Now we believe, not because of your speaking: for we have heard for ourselves, and know that this is indeed the Savior of the world."

And after the two days he went from there to Galilee. For Jesus himself testified, that a prophet has no honor in his own country. So when he came into Galilee, the people received him, having seen all the things that he did in Jerusalem at the feast: for they also went to the feast. He came again to Cana of Galilee, where he made the water wine. And there was a certain nobleman, whose son was sick at Capernaum. When he heard that Jesus had come from Judea to Galilee, he went to him, and begged him that he would come down and heal his son; for he was at the point of death. Jesus said unto him, "Except you see signs and wonders, you will in not believe." The nobleman said to him, "Sir, come down or else my child will die." Jesus said to him, "Go your way; your son lives." The man believed the word that Jesus spoke to him and he went his way. And as he was now going down, his servants met him, saying, that his son lived. So he inquired of them the hour when he began to get well. They said to him, "Yesterday at the seventh hour the fever left him." So the father knew that it was at that hour in which Jesus said to him, "Thy son lives: and himself believed, and his whole house." This is again the second sign that Jesus did, having come out of Judaea into Galilee.

And when the sabbath was past, Mary Magdalene, and Mary the mother of James, and Salome, bought spices, that they might come and anoint him. And very early on the first day of the week, they come to the tomb when the sun was risen. And they were saying among themselves, "Who shall roll us away the stone from the door of the tomb?" and looking up, they see that the stone is rolled back: for it was exceeding great. And entering into the tomb, they saw a young man sitting on the right side, arrayed in a white robe; and they were amazed. And he said to them, "Be not amazed: you seek Jesus, the Nazarene, who has been crucified: He is risen; He is not here: behold, the place where they laid Him! But go, tell his disciples and Peter, He goes before you into Galilee: there shall you see Him, as He said to you." And they went out, and fled from the tomb; for trembling and astonishment had come upon them: and they said nothing to any one; for they were afraid. Now when He was risen early on the first day of the week, He appeared first to Mary Magdalene, from whom He had cast out seven demons. She went and told them that she had been with Him, as they mourned and wept. And they, when they heard that He was alive, and had been seen of her, disbelieved. And after these things He was manifested in another form unto two of them, as they walked, on their way into the country. And they went away and told it unto the rest: neither believed them. And afterward He was manifested unto the eleven themselves as they sat together; and He upbraided them with their unbelief and hardness of heart, because they believed not them that had seen Him after He was risen. And he said unto them, "Go into all the world, and preach the gospel to the whole creation. He that believes and is baptized shall be saved; but he that does not believe shall be condemned. And these signs shall accompany them that believe: in My name shall they cast out demons; they shall speak with new tongues; they shall take up serpents, and if they drink any deadly thing, it shall not hurt them; they shall lay hands on the sick, and they shall recover."

THESE FINAL WORDS OF MARK GIVE scholars pause because there is no evidence that anyone recovered after drinking poison or speaking in new tongues.

So then the Lord Jesus, after He had spoken to them, was received up into heaven, and sat down at the right hand of God. And they went forth, and preached everywhere, the Lord working with them, and confirming the word by the signs that followed.

NOW IN TWO DAYS WAS THE feast of the passover and the feast of unleavened bread, and the chief priests and the scribes sought how they might take Him and kill Him, for they said, "Not during the feast, because there will be tumult of the people." And while He was in Bethany in the house of Simon the leper, as he sat at the table, there came a woman having an alabaster cruse of ointment of pure nard very costly; and she broke the seal, and poured it over His head. But there were some that had indignation among themselves, saying, "To what purpose has this waste of the ointment been made? For this ointment might have been sold for above three hundred shillings, and given to the poor." And they murmured against her. But Jesus said, "Let her alone; why trouble her? She has wrought a good work on me. For you have the poor always with you, and whenever you will you can do them good: but Me you have not always. She has done what she could; she has anointed my body beforehand for the burying.

And verily I say unto you, 'Wherever the gospel shall be preached throughout the whole world, that also which this woman has done shall be spoken of for a memorial of her.'"

And Judas Iscariot, he that was one of the twelve, went away unto the chief priests, that he might deliver Him unto them. And they, when they heard it, were glad, and promised to give him money. And he sought how he might conveniently deliver Him unto them. And on the first day of unleavened bread, when they sacrificed the passover, His disciples said to Him, "Where will You be that we go and make ready that You may eat the passover?" And He sent two of his disciples, and said to them, "Go into the city, and there shall meet you a man bearing a pitcher of water: follow Him; and wherever he shall enter in, say to the master of the house, 'The Teacher says, Where is my guest-chamber, where I shall eat the passover with my disciples?' And he will show you a large upper room furnished and ready: and there make ready for us."

And the disciples went, and came into the city, and found as He had said unto them: and they made ready the passover. And when it was evening He came with the twelve. And as they sat and were eating, Jesus said, "Verily I say to you, 'One of you shall betray Me, *even* he that eats with Me.'" They began to be sorrowful, and to say to Him one by one, "Is it I?" And He said to them, "It is one of the twelve, he that dips with me in the dish. For the Son of man goes, even as it is written of Him: but woe unto that man through whom the Son of man is betrayed! Good were it for that man if he had not been born."

And as they were eating, he took bread, and when he had blessed, He broke it, and gave to them, and said, "Take,: this is my body." And he took a cup, and when he had given thanks, he gave to them: and they all drank of it. And He said unto them, "This is my blood of the covenant, which is poured out for many. Verily I say unto you, 'I shall no more drink of the fruit of the vine, until that day when I drink it new in the kingdom of God.'" And when they had sung a hymn, they went out to the mount of Olives. And Jesus said to them, "All of you shall be offended: for it is written, 'I will smite the shepherd, and the sheep shall be scattered abroad.' However, after I am raised up, I will go before you into Galilee." But Peter said to Him, "Although all shall be offended, but I will not." And Jesus said to Him, "Verily I say unto you, that you to-day, even this night, before the cock crows twice, shall deny me three times." But he spoke vehemently, "If I must die with you, I will not deny you." And in like manner they said the same thing.

And they came to a place which was named Gethsemane: and He said to Hishe saith disciples, "Sit here, while I pray." And He took with Him Peter and James and John, and began to be greatly amazed and very troubled. And He said to them, "My soul is exceeding sorrowful even unto death: stay here, and watch." And He went forward a little, and fell on the ground, and prayed that, if it were possible, the hour might pass away from Him. And he said, "Abba, Father, all things are possible with thee; remove this cup from me: not what I will, but what You will." And He came and found them sleeping, and said to Peter, Simon, "You're sleeping? Could you not watch one hour? Watch and pray, that you enter not into temptation: the spirit indeed is willing, but the flesh is weak."

And again He went away, and prayed, saying the same words. And again He came, and found them sleeping, for their eyes were very heavy; and they knew not what to answer Him. And He came the third time, and said to them, "Sleep on now, and take your rest: it is enough; the hour is come; behold, the Son of man is betrayed into the hands of sinners. Arise, let us be going: behold, he that has betrayed me is at hand." And immediately, while he spoke, came Judas, one of the twelve, and with him a multitude with swords and staves, from the chief priests and the scribes and the elders. Now he that betrayed Him had given them a token, saying, "Whoever I shall kiss, that is He; take Him, and lead Him away safely." And when he came, he said, "Rabbi," and kissed Him. And they laid hands on Him, and took Him. But a certain one of them that stood by drew his sword, and smote the servant of the high priest, and struck off his ear. And Jesus answered and said unto them, "Have you come out, as against a robber, with swords and staves to seize Me? I was daily with you in the temple teaching, and you took me not: but this is done that the scriptures might be fulfilled."

And they all left Him, and fled. And a certain young man followed with Him, having a linen cloth cast about Him, over his naked body: and they lay hold of Him; but he left the linen cloth, and fled naked. And they led Jesus away to the high priest: and there came together with Him all the chief priests and the elders and the scribes. And Peter had followed Him afar off, even within, into the court of the high priest; and he was sitting with the officers, and warming himself in the light of the fire.

Now the chief priests and the whole council sought witness against Jesus to put Him to death; and could not find it. For many bore false witness against Him, and their witness agreed not together. And there stood up certain, and bore false witness against Him. We heard Him say, "I will destroy this temple that is made with hands, and in three days I will build another made without hands." And not even so did their witnesses agree together. And the high priest stood up in the midst, and asked Jesus, saying, "You have nothing to say? What is it which these witness against You?" But He held his peace, and answered nothing. Again the high priest asked Him, and said to Him, "Art thou the Christ, the Son of the Blessed?" And Jesus said, "I am: and you shall see the Son of man sitting at the right hand of Power, and coming with the clouds of heaven." And the high priest rent his clothes, and said, "What further need have we of witnesses? You have heard the blasphemy: what do you think?" And they all condemned Him to be worthy of death. And some began to spit on Him, and to cover his face, and to buffet Him, and to say unto Him, Prophesy: and the officers received Him with blows of their hands. And as Peter was beneath in the court, there came one of the maids of the high priest; and seeing Peter warming Himself, she looked upon Him, and said, "You were also with Jesus." But he denied, saying, "I neither know, nor understand what you are saying," and he went out into the porch; and the cock crew. And the maid saw Him, and began again to say to them that stood by, "This is one of them." But he again denied it. And after a little while again they that stood by said to Peter, "For certain, you are one of them for you are a Galilean." But he began to curse, and to swear, "I know not this man of whom you speak." And immediately the second time the cock crew. And Peter called to mind the word, how that Jesus said to Him, "Before the cock crows twice, you shall deny Me three times." And when he thought about it, he wept.

Then Pilate took Jesus, and scourged him. And the soldiers platted a crown of thorns, and put it on his head, and dressed him in a purple garment; and they came to him, and said, "Hail, King of the Jews!" and they struck him with their hands. And Pilate went out again, and said to the people assembled, "Behold, I bring him out to you, that you may know that I find no crime in him." Jesus came out, wearing the crown of thorns and the purple garment. And Pilate said to them, "Behold, the man!"

When the chief priests and the officers saw him, they cried out, saying, "Crucify him, crucify him!" Pilate said to them, "Take him yourselves, and crucify him: for I find no crime in him." The Jews answered him, "We have a law, and by that law he ought to die, because he made himself the Son of God." When Pilate heard this, he was even more fearful. And he entered into the Praetorium again, and said to Jesus, "Where do you come from?" But Jesus gave him no answer. Pilate said to him, "You won't speak to me? You should know that I have power to release you, and have power to crucify you." Jesus answered him, "You would have no power against me, except it were given to you from above. So he that delivered me to you has the greater sin."

After hearing this, Pilate tried to release him: but the Jews cried out, saying, "If you release this man, you are not Caesar's friend. Every day one that makes himself a king speaks against Caesar." When Pilate heard these words, he brought Jesus out, and sat down on the judgment-seat at a place called The Pavement, but in Hebrew, Gabbatha.

Now it was the Preparation of the passover: it was about the sixth hour. And he said to the Jews, "Behold, your King!" They cried out, "Away with him, away with him, crucify him!" Pilate said to them, "Shall I crucify your King?" The chief priests answered, "We have no king but Caesar." Then he delivered him to them to be crucified. They took Jesus and he went out, bearing the cross for himself, to the place called The place of a skull, which is called in Hebrew, Golgotha: where they crucified him, and with him two others, on either side one, and Jesus in the midst. And Pilate wrote a title also, and put it on the cross. And there was written, JESUS OF NAZARETH, THE KING OF THE JEWS. This title was read many of the Jews, for the place where Jesus was crucified was near the city and it was written in Hebrew and in Latin and in Greek. The chief priests of the Jews said to Pilate, "Write not, The King of the Jews; but that he said, I am King of the Jews." Pilate answered, "What I have written I have written."

The soldiers, when they had crucified Jesus, took his garments and made four parts, to every soldier a part; and also the coat: now the coat was without seam, woven from the top throughout. They said to one to another, "Let us not rend it, but cast lots for it, whose it shall be: that the scripture might be fulfilled, which says, 'They parted my garments among them, And upon my vesture did they cast lots.'" These things the soldiers did. But there were standing by the cross of Jesus his mother, and his mother's sister, Mary the wife of Clopas, and Mary Magdalene.

When Jesus saw his mother, and the disciple standing by whom he loved, he said to his mother, "Woman, behold your son!" Then he said to the disciples, "Behold! My mother!" And from that hour the disciple took her to his own home. After this Jesus, knowing that all things are now finished, that the scripture might be accomplished, said, "I thirst." There was set there a vessel full of vinegar: so they put a sponge full of the vinegar upon hyssop, and brought it to his mouth. When Jesus had received the vinegar, he said, "It is finished," and he bowed his head, and gave up his spirit.

The Jews, because it was the Preparation, that the bodies should not remain on the cross upon the sabbath (for the day of that sabbath was a high day), asked of Pilate that their legs might be broken, and that they might be taken away. The soldiers came, and broke the legs of the first, and of the other that was crucified with him: but when they came to Jesus, and saw that he was dead already, they didn't brake his legs. One of the soldiers with a spear pierced his side, and immediately there came out blood and water. And he that has seen this has borne witness, and his witness is true: and he knows that he speaks the truth, that you, also, may believe. For these things came to pass, that the scripture might be fulfilled, A bone of him shall not be broken. And again another scripture says, They shall look on him whom they pierced.

And after these things Joseph of Arimathaea, being a disciple of Jesus, but secretly for fear of the Jews, asked of Pilate that he might take away the body of Jesus: and Pilate gave him permission. So he came and took away his body. And Nicodemus also came, he who at the first came to him by night, bringing a mixture of myrrh and aloes, about a hundred pounds. So they took the body of Jesus, and bound it in linen cloths with the spices, as the custom of the Jews is to bury. Now in the place where he was crucified there was a garden; and in the garden a new tomb that had never been used. Then because of the Jews' Preparation (for the tomb was nigh at hand) they laid Jesus.

Now after the Sabbath, as it began to dawn toward the first day of the week, Mary Magdalene and the other Mary came to look at the grave. And behold, a severe earthquake had occurred, for an angel of the Lord descended from heaven and came and rolled away the stone and sat upon it. And his appearance was like lightning, and his clothing as white as snow. The guards shook for fear of Him and became like dead men. The angel said to the women, "Do not be afraid; for I know that you are looking for Jesus who has been crucified."

How did these two women know the location of Jesus' grave? Earlier in Matthew's account he tells us that these same two women had watched Joseph seal the tomb with a large stone, also that Pilate had instructed the Pharisees to post their own guard at the tomb, which they did after affixing to it a seal. The Pharisees feared that Jesus' followers would come and take His body in order to promote the myth of His resurrection. Matthew records a supernatural event in these verses, as regards rolling away the stone. Mark tells the story a bit differently by writing that the women saw that the stone had been rolled away and that an angel was waiting for them, inside the tomb; presumably, it was the angel who had moved the stone. Luke tells us only that the two women saw that the stone had been moved. And John reports that only Mary Magdalene was a witness to the event. It's an example of something we already know: each writer tells the story in his own way.

"He is not here, for He has risen, just as He said. Come, see the place where He was lying. Go quickly and tell His disciples that He has risen from the dead; and behold, He is going ahead of you into Galilee, there you will see Him; behold, I have told you."

And they left the tomb quickly with fear and great joy and ran to report it to His disciples. And behold, Jesus met them and greeted them. And they came up and took hold of His feet and worshiped Him. Then Jesus said to them, "Do not be afraid; go and take word to My brethren to leave for Galilee, and there they will see Me." Now while they were on their way, some of the guard came into the city and reported to the chief priests all that had happened. And when they had assembled with the elders and consulted together, they gave a large sum of money to the soldiers, and said, "You are to say, 'His disciples came by night and stole Him away while we were asleep.' And if this should come to the governor's ears, we will win Him over and keep you out of trouble." And they took the money and did as they had been instructed; and this story was widely spread among the Jews, and is to this day. But the eleven disciples proceeded to Galilee, to the mountain which Jesus had designated. When they saw Him, they worshiped Him; but some were doubtful.

And Jesus came up and spoke to them, saying, "All authority has been given to Me in heaven and on earth. Go therefore and make disciples of all the nations, baptizing them in the name of the Father and the Son and the Holy Spirit, teaching them to observe all that I commanded you; and lo, I am with you always, even to the end of the age."

This is the so-called Great Commission and it appears only in Matthew's gospel. These may be Jesus' most important words because they establish the legitimacy of, and the need for, Christianity and its church.

John Sager is a retired United States Intelligence officer whose services for the CIA, in various capacities, spanned more than a half-century. A widower, he makes his home in the Covenant Shores retirement community, on Mercer Island, Washington.